KINGST

3 3338 00131 0312

P9-DGM-373

PENGUIN BOOKS

RIDING IN CARS WITH BOYS

Beverly Donofrio studied at Weslyan University, then went on to receive an MFA in creative writing from Columbia University. Her work has appeared in *The Village Voice* and *New York* magazine. She is also the author of *Looking for Mary*. She lives in Mexico.

DISCARD

DISCARD

RIDING IN CARS WITH BOYS

CONFESSIONS OF A BAD GIRL WHO MAKES GOOD

BEVERLY DONOFRIO

PENGUIN BOOKS

PENGUIN BOOKS

Published by the Penguin Group
Penguin Putnam Inc., 375 Hudson Street,
New York, New York 10014, U.S.A.
Penguin Books Ltd, 27 Wrights Lane, London W8 5TZ, England
Penguin Books Australia Ltd, Ringwood, Victoria, Australia
Penguin Books Canada Ltd, 10 Alcorn Avenue,
Toronto, Ontario, Canada M4V 3B2
Penguin Books (N.Z.) Ltd, 182–190 Wairau Road,
Auckland 10, New Zealand

Penguin Books Ltd, Registered Offices: Harmondsworth, Middlesex, England

First published in the United States of America by
William Morrow and Company, Inc., 1990
Published in Penguin Books 1992
This edition published 2001

1 3 5 7 9 10 8 6 4 2

Copyright © Beverly Donofrio, 1990
All rights reserved

Portions of this work have appeared in different form in *The Village Voice*.

Grateful acknowledgement is made for permission
to reprint lyrics from the following:
"Do You Know the Way to San Jose" Hal David, Burt Bacharach Copyright ©
1967 by Blue Seas Music, Inc., & JAC Music Co., Inc. All rights reserved.
"All I Want" Joni Mitchell Copyright © 1971, 1975 by Joni Mitchell
Publishing Corp. All rights reserved. Used by permission.
"Love Child" R. Dean Taylor, Frank Wilson, Pamela Sawyer, Dennis Lussler
Copyright © 1968 by Jobete Music Co., Inc., & Stone Agate Music

THE LIBRARY OF CONGRESS HAS CATALOGED
THE HARDCOVER EDITION AS FOLLOWS:
Donofrio, Beverly.
Riding in cars with boys: confessions of
a bad girl who makes good/Beverly Donofrio.
p. cm.
ISBN 0-688-08337-4 (hc.)
ISBN 0 14 02.9629 8 (pbk)
I. Title.
PS3554.O536R5 1990
813'.54—dc21   89–78126

Printed in the United States of America
Set in Bembo • Designed by Jaye Zimet

Except in the United States of America, this book is sold subject
to the condition that it shall not, by way of trade or otherwise, be lent,
re-sold, hired out, or otherwise circulated without the publisher's prior
consent in any form of binding or cover other than that in which it
is published and without a similar condition including this
condition being imposed on the subsequent purchaser.

To my mother, my father, and my son

This book would not exist without the help, encouragement, and affection of my teachers Richard Price and Tony Connor; Dr. Joseph Finkle; my agent Gail Hochman; my editors Jim Landis and Jane Meara; and my good friends Robin Tewes, Terry Reed, Sheryl Lukomski, Kirsten Dehner, Trudy Dittmar, Janet Donofrio Rieth, Peter Alson, Alex Kotlowitz, and Thomas deMaar.

Prologue

I'M driving my son to college. It's dark and pouring rain out. I always imagined it would be sunny, like after a storm, magnificent puffs of clouds moving a hundred miles a minute across an electric blue sky. And there I'd be, hanging out a window, waving my arms and shouting hallelujah as my son disappeared around a corner. I thought it would feel like Bastille Day did for the starving French masses. But instead of a freedom frenzy, I'm having a nervous breakdown.

A few days ago I saw this kid on the uptown bus. He was dangling a GI Joe from his mouth as he dug in his backpack, then pulled out some drawings to show to his mother. He watched her face as she placed the pictures on her knees, smoothed them with her hands and smiled. The scene made me blubber. I know everybody cries when their kid goes to college. But this was not supposed to happen to me. I was not supposed to be driving in a downpour, mumbling, "Oh God," and using every molecule of will in my body to keep from crying.

I was not supposed to have a kid to begin with.

I try to pass a bully truck. A gust of air pushes me to the edge of a lane and sprays water on our little Honda, so the windshield floods and I can't see

9

through it for a second. Jason grabs the handle on the dashboard and closes his eyes—not hysterical, but indulgent. He thinks I'm a terrible driver, a notion he picked up when he was seven and eight and nine and I'd fly over bumps to make him scream or slam on the brakes for no reason except I loved to scare him. When he was four, I soaped up my face, then scrinched it into a horrifying grimace and chased him screaming through the house. Lately, I've been thinking of the things I did and feeling like a maniac mother. Lately, I've been looking at my life like there's something to learn.

I look at my son as he pushes buttons on the radio. How could I have raised such a kid? He's tall and handsome and calm. Mostly calm. That's what you think when you see him. You think, That kid's got self-possession. Like Jimmy Stewart or maybe Gary Cooper. People say I'm lucky, but I always thought different.

I hear Frank Sinatra singing "My Way." I tell Jase to stop there and I think, That's it. I wasn't a terrible person. I just did like Frank Sinatra. Then a picture of Sid Vicious singing the same song comes to mind and makes me feel awful all over again.

PART
ONE

CHAPTER 1

TROUBLE began in 1963. I'm not blaming it on President Kennedy's assassination or its being the beginning of the sixties or the Vietnam War or the Beatles or the make-out parties in the fallout shelters all over my hometown of Wallingford, Connecticut, or my standing in line with the entire population of Dag Hammarskjold Junior High School and screaming when a plane flew overhead because we thought it was the Russians. These were not easy times, it's true. But it's too convenient to pin the trouble that would set me on the path of most resistance on the times.

The trouble I'm talking about was my first real trouble, the age-old trouble. The getting in trouble as in "Is she in Trouble?" trouble. As in pregnant. As in the girl who got pregnant in high school. In the end that sentence for promiscuous behavior, that penance (to get Catholic here for a minute, which I had the fortune or misfortune of being, depending on the way you look at it)—that kid of mine, to be exact—would turn out to be a blessing instead of a curse. But I had no way of knowing it at the time and, besides, I'm getting ahead of myself.

By 1963, the fall of the eighth grade, I was ready. I was hot to trot. My hair was teased to basketball dimensions, my 16 oz. can of Miss Clairol hairspray was tucked into my shoulder bag. Dominic Mezzi whistled between his teeth every time I passed him in the hallway, and the girls from the project—the ones with boys' initials scraped into their forearms, then colored with black ink—smiled and said hi when they saw me. I wore a padded bra that lifted my tits to inches below my chin, and my father communicated to me only through my mother. "Mom," I said. "Can I go to the dance at the Y on Friday?"

"It's all right with me, but you know your father."

Yes, I knew my father. Mr. Veto, the Italian cop, who never talked and said every birthday, "So, how old're you anyway? What grade you in this year?" It was supposed to be a joke, but who could tell if he really knew or was just covering? I mean, the guy stopped looking at me at the first appearance of my breasts, way back in the fifth grade.

In the seventh grade, I began to suspect he was spying on me, when I had my run-in with Danny Dempsey at Wilkinson's Theater. Danny Dempsey was a high school dropout and a hood notorious in town for fighting. I was waiting in the back of the seats after the lights dimmed for my best friend, Donna Wilhousky, to come back with some candy when this Danny Dempsey sidled up to me and leaned his shoulder into mine. Then he reached in his pocket and pulled out a knife, which he laid in the palm of his hand, giving it a little tilt so it glinted in the screen light. I pressed my back against the wall as far away from the knife as I could, and got goosebumps. Then Donna showed up with a pack of Banana Splits and Mint Juleps, and Danny Dempsey backed away. For weeks, every time the phone rang I prayed it was Danny Dempsey. That

was about the time my father started acting suspicious

whenever I set foot out of his house. He was probably just smelling the perfume of budding sexuality on me and was acting territorial, like a dog. Either that or maybe his buddy Skip Plotkin, the official cop of Wilkinson's Theater, had filed a report on me.

Which wasn't a bad idea when I think of it, because I was what you call boy crazy. It probably started with Pat Boone when I was four years old. I went to see him in the movie where he sang "Bernadine" with his white bucks thumping and his fingers snapping, and I was in love. From that day on whenever "Bernadine" came on the radio, I swooned, spun around a couple of times, then dropped in a faked-dead faint. I guess my mother thought this was cute because she went out and bought me the forty-five. Then every day after kindergarten, I ran straight to the record player for my dose, rocked my head back and forth, snapped my fingers like Pat Boone, then when I couldn't stand it another second, I swooned, spun around, and dropped in a faked-dead faint.

I was never the type of little girl who hated boys. Never. Well, except for my brother. I was just the oldest of three girls, while he was the Oldest, plus the only boy in an Italian family, and you know what that means: golden penis. My father sat at one end of the table and my brother sat at the other, while my mother sat on the sidelines with us girls. You could say I resented him a little. I had one advantage though—the ironclad rule. My brother, because he was a boy, was not allowed to lay one finger on us girls. So when his favorite show came on the TV, I stood in front of it. And when he said, "Move," I said, "Make me," which he couldn't.

But other boys could chase me around the yard for hours dangling earthworms from their fingers, or call me Blackie at the bus stop when my skin was tanned dirt-brown after the summer, or forbid me to set foot in their tent or play in their soft-, kick-, or dodgeball games. They could chase me away when I tried to follow them into the woods, their bows slung over their shoulders and their hatchets tucked into their belts. And I still liked them, which is not to say I didn't get back at them. The summer they all decided to ban girls, meaning me and Donna, from their nightly softball games in the field behind our houses, Donna and I posted signs on telephone poles announcing the time of the inoculations they must receive to qualify for teams. On the appointed day they stood in line at Donna's cellar door. Short ones, tall ones, skinny and fat, they waited their turn, then never even winced when we pricked their skin with a needle fashioned from a pen and a pin.

By the summer of 1963, my boy craziness had reached such a pitch that I was prepared to sacrifice the entire summer to catch a glimpse of Denny Winters, the love of my and Donna's life. Donna and I walked two miles to his house every day, then sat under a big oak tree across the street, our transistor radio between us, and stared at his house, waiting for some movement, a sign of life, a blind pulled up or down, a curtain shunted aside, a door opening, a dog barking. Anything. Denny's sister, who was older and drove a car, sometimes drove off and sometimes returned. But that was it. In an entire summer of vigilance, we never saw Denny Winters arrive or depart. Maybe he had mononucleosis; maybe he was away at camp. We never saw him mow the lawn or throw a ball against the house for practice.

What we did see was a lot of teenage boys sitting low in cars, cruising by. Once in a while, a carload would whistle, flick a cigarette into the gutter at our feet, and sing, "Hello, girls." Whenever they did that, Donna and I stuck our chins in the air and turned our heads away. "Stuck up," they hollered.

But we knew the cars to watch for: the blue-and-white Chevy with the blond boy driving, the forest-green Pontiac with the dark boy, the white Rambler, the powder-blue Camaro, the yellow Falcon. I decided that when I finally rode in a car with a boy, I wouldn't sit right next to him like I was stuck with glue to his armpit. I'd sit halfway there—just to the right of the radio, maybe.

My father, however, had other ideas. My father forbade me to ride in cars with boys until I turned sixteen. That was the beginning.

"I hate him," I cried to my mother when my father was out of the house.

"Well, he thinks he's doing what's best for you," she said.

"What? Keeping me prisoner?"

"You know your father. He's suspicious. He's afraid you'll get in trouble."

"What kind of trouble?"

"You'll ruin your reputation. You're too young. Boys think they can take advantage. Remember what I told you. If a boy gets fresh, just cross your legs."

It was too embarrassing. I changed the subject. "I hate him," I repeated.

By the time I turned fourteen, the next year, I was speeding around Wallingford in crowded cars with guys who took corners on two wheels, flew over bumps, and skidded down the road to get me screaming. Whenever I saw a cop car, I lay down on the seat, out of sight.

While I was still at Dag Hammarskjold Junior High

School, I got felt up in the backseat of a car, not because I wanted to exactly, but because I was only fourteen and thought that when everybody else was talking about making out, it meant they got felt up. That was the fault of two girls from the project, Penny Calhoun and Donna DiBase, who were always talking about their periods in front of boys by saying their *friend* was staying over for a week and how their *friend* was a *bloody mess*. They told me that making out had three steps: kissing, getting felt up, and then Doing It. Next thing I knew, I was at the Church of the Resurrection bazaar and this cute little guy with a Beatles haircut sauntered up and said, "I've got a sore throat. Want to go for a ride to get some cough drops?" I hesitated. I didn't even know his name, but then the two girls I was with, both sophomores in high school, said, "Go! Are you crazy? That's Skylar Barrister, the president of the sophomore class." We ended up with two other couples parked by the dump. My face was drooly with saliva (step one) when "A Hard Day's Night" came on the radio and Sky placed a hand on one of my breasts (step two). Someone must've switched the station, because "A Hard Day's Night" was on again when his hand started moving up the inside of my thigh. I crossed my legs like my mother said, but he uncrossed them. Lucky for me, there was another couple in the backseat and Sky Barrister was either too afraid or had good enough manners not to involve them in the loss of my virginity or I really would've been labeled a slut. Not that my reputation wasn't ruined anyway, because sweetheart Sky broadcast the news that Beverly Donofrio's easy—first to his friends at the country club and then, exponentially, to the entire town. Hordes of boys called me up after that. My father was beside himself. I was grounded. I couldn't talk on the phone for more than a minute. My mother tried to intervene. "Sonny," she said. "You have to trust her."

"I know what goes on with these kids. I see it every day, and you're going to tell me?"

"What's talking on the phone going to hurt?" my mother asked.

"You heard what I said. I don't want to hear another word about it. You finish your phone call in a minute, miss, or I hang it up on you. You hear me?"

I heard him loud and clear, and it was okay with me—for a while, anyway, because my love of boys had turned sour. Sophomore year in high school, my English class was across the hall from Sky Barrister's and every time I walked by, there was a disturbance—a chitter, a laugh—coming from the guys he stood with. My brother was the captain of the football team and I wished he was the type who'd slam Sky Barrister against a locker, maybe knock a couple of his teeth out, but not my brother. My brother was the type who got a good-citizenship medal for never missing a single day of high school.

Meanwhile, his sister began to manifest definite signs of being a bad girl. My friends and I prided ourselves on our foul mouths and our stunts, like sitting across from the jocks' table in the cafeteria and giving the guys crotch shots, then when they started elbowing each other and gawking, we shot them the finger and slammed our knees together. Or we collected gingerbread from lunch trays and molded them into shapes like turds and distributed them in water fountains.

The thing was, we were sick to death of boys having all the fun, so we started acting like them: We got drunk in the parking lot before school dances and rode real low in cars, elbows stuck out windows, tossing beer cans, flicking butts, and occasionally pulling down our pants and shaking our fannies at passing vehicles.

But even though we were very busy showing the world that girls could have fun if only they'd stop acting nice, eventually it troubled us all that the type of boys we liked—collegiate, popular, seniors—wouldn't touch us with a ten-foot pole.

One time I asked a guy in the Key Club why no guys liked me. "Am I ugly or stupid or something?"

"No." He scratched under his chin. "It's probably the things you say."

"What things?"

"I don't know."

"You think it's because I don't put out?"

"See? You shouldn't say things like that to a guy."

"Why?"

"It's not right."

"But why?"

"I don't know."

"Come on, is it because it's not polite or because it's about sex or because it embarrasses you? Tell me."

"You ask too many questions. You analyze too much, that's your problem."

To say that I analyzed too much is not to say I did well in school. Good grades, done homework—any effort abruptly ended in the tenth grade, when my mother laid the bad news on me that I would not be going to college. It was a Thursday night. I was doing the dishes, my father was sitting at the table doing a paint-by-numbers, and we were humming "Theme from Exodus" together. My mother was wiping the stove before she left for work at Bradlees, and for some reason she was stinked—maybe she had her period, or maybe it was because my father and I always hummed while I did the dishes and she was jealous. Neither of us acknowledged that we were basically harmonizing. It was more like it was just an accident that we were humming the same song. Our favorites were "'Bye 'Bye Blackbird," "Sentimental Journey," "Tonight," and "Exodus." After "Exodus," I said, "Hey, Ma. I was thinking I want to go to U Conn instead of Southern or Central. It's harder to get into, but it's a better school."

"And who's going to pay for it?"

It's odd that I never thought about the money, especially since my parents were borderline paupers and being poor was my mother's favorite topic. I just figured, naively, that anybody who was smart enough could go to college.

"I don't know. Aren't there loans or something?"

"Your father and I have enough bills. You better stop dreaming. Take typing. Get a *good* job when you graduate."

"I'm not going to be a secretary."

She lifted a burner and swiped under it. "We'll see," she said.

"I'm moving to New York."

"Keep dreaming." She dropped the burner back down.

So I gritted my teeth and figured I'd have to skip college and go straight to Broadway, but it pissed me off. Because I wasn't simply a great actress, I was smart too. I'd known this since the seventh grade, when I decided my family was made up of a bunch of morons with lousy taste in television. I exiled myself into the basement recreation room every night to get away from them. There were these hairy spiders down there, and I discovered if I dropped a Book of Knowledge on them they'd fist up into dots, dead as doornails. Then one night after a spider massacre, I opened a book up and discovered William Shakespeare—his quality-of-mercy soliloquy, to be exact. Soon I'd read everything in the books by him, and then by Whitman and Tennyson and Shelley. I memorized Hamlet's soliloquy and said it to the mirror behind the bar. To do this in the seventh grade made me think I was a genius. And now, to be told by my mother, who'd never read a book in her life, that I couldn't go to college was worse than infuriating, it was unjust. Somebody would have to pay.

That weekend my friends and I went around throwing eggs at passing cars. We drove through Choate, the ritzy prep school in the middle of town, and I had an inspiration. "Stop the car," I said. "Excuse me," I said to a little sports-jacketed Choatie crossing Christian Street. "Do you know where Christian Street is?"

"I'm not sure," he said, "but I think it's that street over there." He pointed to the next road over.

"You're standing on it, asshole!" I yelled, flinging an egg at the name tag on his jacket. I got a glimpse of his face as he watched the egg drool down his chest and I'll remember the look of disbelief as it changed to sadness till the day I die. We peeled out, my friends hooting and hollering and slapping me on the back.

I thought I saw a detective car round the bend and follow us down the street, but it was just my imagination. Now that my father'd been promoted from a regular cop to a detective, it was worse. Believe me, being a bad girl and having my father cruising around in an unmarked vehicle was no picnic. One time, I'd dressed up as a pregnant woman, sprayed gray in my hair, and bought a quart of gin, then went in a motorcade to the bonfire before the big Thanksgiving football game. We had the windows down even though it was freezing out and were singing "Eleanor Rigby" when we slammed into the car in front of us and the car in back slammed into us—a domino car crash. We all got out; there was no damage except a small dent in Ronald Kovacs's car in front. He waved us off, and we went to the bonfire.

Back home, I went directly to the bathroom to brush my teeth when the phone rang. In a minute my mother called, "Bev, your father's down the station. He wants to see you."

My heart stalled. "What about?"

"You know him. He never tells me anything."

I looked at myself in the mirror and said, "You are not drunk. You have not been drinking. You have done nothing wrong, and if that man accuses you, you have every reason in the world to be really mad." This was the Stanislavsky method of lying, and it worked wonders. I considered all my lying invaluable practice for the stage. There were countless times that I maintained not only a straight but a sincere face as my mother made me put one hand on the Bible, the other on my heart, and swear that I hadn't done something it was evident to the entire world only I could have done.

My father sat me in a small green room, where he took a seat behind a desk. "You were drinking," he said.

"No I wasn't," I said.

"You ever hear of Ronald Kovacs?"

"Yes. We were in a three-car collision. He slammed on his brakes in the middle of the motorcade, and we hit him."

"It's always the driver in the back's fault, no matter what the car in front does. That's the law. Maybe your friend wasn't paying too much attention. Maybe you were all loaded."

"You always think the worst. Somebody hit us from behind too, you know."

"Who was driving your car?"

"I'm not a rat like that jerk Kovacs."

"That's right. Be a smart ass. See where it gets you. I already know who was operating the vehicle. You better be straight with me or your friend, the driver, might end up pinched. It was Beatrice?"

"Yes."

"She wasn't drinking but you were?"

"*No*! Did you ever think that maybe Ronald Kovacs was drinking? Did you ever think that maybe he's trying to cover his own ass?"

"Watch your language."

I put on my best injured look and pretended to be choking back tears. It was easy because I was scared to death. Cops kept passing in the hall outside the door to the office. I was going out on a limb. If they found concrete evidence that I'd been drinking, my father would really be embarrassed. He might hit me when we got home, and I'd definitely be grounded, probably for the rest of my life.

"They're setting up the lie detector in the other room. We got it down from Hartford for a case we been working on," he said. "Will you swear on the lie detector that you're telling the truth?"

A bead of sweat dripped down my armpit. "Good. And bring in Ronald Kovacs and make him take it, too. Then you'll see who's a liar."

Turns out there was no lie detector; it was a bluff and I'd won the gamble.

When I got home, I played it for all it was worth with my mother. "He never trusts me. He always believes the worst. I can't stand it. How could you have married him?"

"You know your father. It's his nature to be suspicious."

"I wish he worked at the steel mill."

"You and me and the man in the moon. Then maybe I could pay the doctor bills. But that's not your father. He wanted to be a cop and make a difference. He didn't want to punch a time clock and have a boss looking over his shoulder."

When I was four, before my father became a cop, he pumped gas at the garage on the corner, and every day I brought him sandwiches in a paper bag. He'd smile like I'd just brightened his day when he saw me, then I sat on his lap while he ate. Sometimes I fell asleep, leaning my head against his chest, lulled by the warmth of his body and the rumble of trucks whooshing past. Sometimes I traced the red-and-green American Beauty rose on his forearm. I thought that flower was the most beautiful thing in the world back then. Now it was gray as newsprint, and whenever I caught a glimpse of it, I turned my eyes.

"You should've told him not to be a cop," I said. "It's ruining my life."

"It's not up to the wife to tell the husband what to do," my mother said.

"He tells you what to do all the time."

"The man wears the pants in the family."

"I'm never getting married."

"You'll change your tune."

"And end up like you? Never in a million years."

"You better not let your father catch you talking to me like that."

CHAPTER 2

MAYBE it was poetic justice for being so contemptuous of my mother and her position in life—as my father's servant—that landed me, before I graduated high school, at the altar.

I met Sonny Raymond Bouchard on New Year's Eve in the eleventh grade. As usual, I didn't have a date and neither did my best friend, Fay Johnston. Her parents were away for the weekend, so I was sleeping over. We were drinking gin and Fresca in martini glasses and pretending we were rich and famous and living in New York City when her brother Cal showed up with two of his hoody friends, Lizard and Raymond. I'd heard about a friend of Cal's named Raymond and how his brother was in jail for holding up Cumberland Farms with a gun. Raymond's hair was black and greased high back. He wore tight black pants and pointy black shoes.

Cal crammed a case of Colt 45 in the refrigerator, then stood in the doorway of the living room and said, "Happy New Year!" as he slammed his heels together and pointed a can of beer in the air like a Nazi salute. Then the three of them came into the living room and started talking about Lizard's giving a guy at the Farm Shop a bloody nose.

"Why'd you hit him? What did he do?" I asked.

"Nothing," Lizard said.

"He ranked on Lizard's sister," Raymond said, opening a beer.

"Called her a douche bag." Cal giggled.

I liked that. Hoods had their drawbacks—like using *dems* and *dose* when they spoke and wearing their hair like Elvis's—but usually they weren't afraid to fight for a girl's honor.

Ray took a long drink of beer, and when he put the can down, his eyes landed on me. Then Cal put "Sunny" on the record player. It skipped: "Sunny, thank you for the . . . Sunny, thank you for the . . . Sunny, thank you for the . . ." Cal said, "First one to change the record's a pussy."

This went on for ten minutes. I kept an eye on Ray to see how he was taking the torture. That's when I noticed he smoked Lucky Strikes, like my father. I wondered what he was thinking. He sat still in the chair like the Lincoln Memorial, except every once in a while when he lifted a heel off the floor then put it back down. I wondered if he carried a gun like his brother. I figured he could probably fix cars because that's why hoods were called greasers.

Cal flung his shoe at the record.

"Eh-heh," Fay said. "Cal's a pussy."

"Shut up, chicken legs." He swigged his beer.

"Drop dead, raisin nuts." She threw a pillow at him, knocking his beer in a gush across the carpet.

Fay stood up and dropped into Lizard's lap. He was called Lizard because he'd eat any kind of insect. Only thing was, it had to be living. Fay didn't care who she flirted with.

"Do my bones dig into you when I sit on your lap, Liz?" Fay said.

"You're light as a bird."

"Do you think I'm too skinny?"

"Nah, you're just right."

I knew she was thinking, Well, you're fat as an ox and ugly as sin or something like that. Fay was always flirting with guys who didn't have a chance in hell. Usually, I thought it was mean, but this night I thought maybe she had the right idea, so the next time I returned from the kitchen with a gin and Fresca, I coasted into Raymond's lap and said, "Hi, I'm Beverly."

"Raymond." He nodded and shifted his weight. I suggested we move to the sofa.

"I never saw you around school," I said.

"Quit."

"Why?"

"Buy a car."

"Your parents didn't care?"

"Nope." He stretched and laid an arm across my shoulder. I thought of Danny Dempsey and wondered if Raymond carried a knife. I put my head on his shoulder and interrogated him.

"So, you have a job?"

"Yep."

"What do you do?"

"Work down Cyanamid. Is your old man the cop?"

"Yes. I hate him. Is your brother really in jail?"

"Yep."

"For what?"

"Armed robbery."

"That's terrible. Did your mother cry when she found out?"

"Yeah." He kept flicking his thumb with his index finger. I took his hand in my lap to hold it still.

"What about your father?" I asked.

"He don't know. He ain't been around for a couple of years."

"Where is he?"

"Bowery."

"In New York?"

"He's a drunk."

Raymond was a high school dropout, his brother was a thief in jail, and his father was a Bowery bum. He needed me. More than anything else in the world I wanted Raymond to cry on my shoulder. I kissed his forehead. He pulled his face away and kissed my mouth.

It would be like *On the Waterfront*. He'd be Marlon Brando and I'd be Eva Marie Saint. I'd tutor Raymond for his high school equivalency; he'd listen to me recite Shakespearean soliloquys in my cellar. Pretty soon he'd wear crewneck sweaters and loafers. He was lying on top of me. It was probably too late to turn back now: I had a hood for a boyfriend.

By the time Raymond and I came up for air, the room was deserted. I told Ray I had to go to the bathroom, and as soon as I sat on the toilet, Fay barged in. "What are you doing? You like Sonny?" she said.

"I think so."

"I don't believe it."

"Tell me about him."

"What's to tell? He was the neighborhood simp. We never let him play baseball and shit because he was such a slug. Used to call him spider after a hairy mole he had growing under his earlobe. Teased him so much he had it removed, surgically."

"Poor Raymond." I flushed the toilet.

"Sonny Bouchard is retarded, Beverly." She sat on the toilet. "I can't believe you like him. Are you sleeping with him on the couch?"

"I guess so."

"Have fun." She flushed the toilet and walked out.

When I went back to Raymond, I looked for the

mole scar. It was a silvery patch the size of a quarter beneath his earlobe. I kissed it and we lay down. I told him I hated the name Sonny and would always call him Raymond. Soon he was breathing regularly and I slid off the couch, tiptoed outside, and stood on the carport. There was no moon, but the sky was heavy with stars. My breath puffed white clouds and there was no sound except for I-91 in the distance. I walked to Fay's window and tapped it. She got up and opened it. "What're you, crazy? It's freezing out."

"Nice though." I spread my arms to demonstrate.

In a minute she stood beside me, a blanket around her shoulders. She wrapped me in. "Let's walk," I suggested.

The grass cracked under my bare feet. When we stepped onto the main road, a car whizzed by beeping. Soon it would be light out. I spotted a red flag sticking up on a mailbox. I pushed it down, then back up, and without thinking about it, I bent it back and forth until it snapped off in my hand. "Wow," Fay said. She went across the street and did the same. We hurried around the block breaking off every flag in sight, until we'd circled back to her house. We had about thirty of them wrapped in the pouch of our blanket. "What'll we do with them?" I said.

"I don't know." Fay hugged herself. "I bet we could get arrested."

"Willful destruction of federal property or some shit."

"I know," she said. I followed her into a vacant lot. She knelt down on the ground and banged a flag in with a rock. I hammered in the next one. We made a circle of red flags in the middle of the field, then stood for a long time looking.

"Maybe no one will touch them," she said.

"Maybe they'll be here forever." I shivered.

One year later, almost to the day, I was shivering again, this time from nerves. I was in Fay's bedroom and at one o'clock on the dot, I dialed the phone to find out if I was pregnant. I dropped the phone and fell face first on the bed.

"Well, what did they say?" Fay asked.

"Positive."

"Postitive? What does positive mean?"

"Pregnant."

"But it could mean you're positively not pregnant, couldn't it?"

"Could it?"

"Call them back and ask."

"You call."

I slid onto the floor and rested my forehead on her knees as she dialed. She hung up and said, "You're fucked."

I broke the news to Raymond that night as we sat at the drive-in, the little portable heater between us on the seat, a motorcycle movie called *The Wild Angels* (Raymond's all-time favorite) on the screen.

"Raymond," I said. "Our lives are ruined."

"Don't you love me?"

"Yes. But still. I mean, why'd this happen to us? Why me? Do you think I have bad luck?"

"You probably got it from me. I told you you shouldn't love me. I'm trouble."

Raymond always said things like that. In the beginning, it made me hug him and kiss him. The first time I'd said "I love you" was when he was drunk and crying. It was in response to his saying, "You shouldn't love me." Now his self-pity just made me mad. Possibly because I was thinking he was right, I shouldn't love him, because if I hadn't, I wouldn't be sitting at a stupid motorcycle movie, pregnant.

But what I said was, "Don't say that," then changed the subject to other depressing topics. "You're going to have to work so hard," I said. "You wanted to quit. Now you can't."

"I'll get another job maybe."

He didn't seem nearly upset enough. "We can't spend any money," I said. "We have to save everything."

He nodded his head, then at intermission he bought hot dogs, sodas, and fries, and I got furious at him for spending the money. But I ate my hot dog, my fries, and half his fries anyway. I was starving.

For the next month, behind Raymond's back, I bumped my ass down stairs, punched myself in the stomach, and threw myself from couch to floor ten times every night before bed. Anything. Anything was better than telling my parents, especially my father, that I'd been screwing Raymond in the basement recreation room while he sat above me watching television in his reclining chair every night. How could I mention the word *sex* to him when I couldn't stay in the same room through a Playtex living bra commercial?

It was 1968 and abortion wasn't legal. If I'd known you could get one in Puerto Rico, I'd have sold my onyx ring, opal necklace, and Raymond's canary-yellow Bonneville to get there. Fact was, I never really thought about the baby, pictured it or imagined being a mother. I was too worried about telling my parents. And I was depressed, despondent, deeply disappointed. I always thought it was my destiny to become a star. But now I'd be married to Raymond for the rest of my life. I'd be a housewife with no money, a station wagon, and a husband whose intellectual curiosity could be summed up in his favorite expression: How come dat?

It seemed to me that God or the will of the world or fate or whatever it is that determines a person's life had turned against me. It's true I'd been the first of my friends to lose my virginity, but within a week of my breaking the news, three of them had followed suit. Now we were trading how-to-have-orgasm tips and none of *them* was pregnant. Fay had even been given a third-of-a-carat diamond and was due to marry a twenty-six-year-old sailor stationed on a nuclear submarine a week after graduation. Why was it my lot in life to be singled out for public humiliation?

Every night for that long month I lay on my stomach on the sofa saying, Next commercial, I'll tell my parents next commercial, but I never could make the words come out of my mouth. So finally, on my way to school one Monday morning, I left a note in the mailbox saying, "Dear Mom and Dad, I'm really sorry. I know I've disappointed you I'm pregnant. Love, your daughter Beverly.

School that day was a nightmare. As if I didn't have enough on my mind, Mr. O'Rourke, the history teacher, decided to notice I was alive and pick on me. "Miss Donofrio," he said.

I didn't hear him.

"Miss Donofrio, I hate to interrupt whatever you're doing [I was cleaning out my pocketbook]. We were talking about Andrew Jackson, a president I'm sure in your vast wisdom you have a good deal of respect for." The class snickered. "I was wondering if you would do us the favor of shedding some light on the subject. Tell us anything, anything at all, about Mr. Jackson."

"I don't know anything."

"What a pity. Then I must assume you didn't read the assignment. I think you'd better write me two pages on the topic."

"You want me to tell you anything?"

"That's what I said."

"He was a president. He wore a white wig."

"Not good enough."

"You said anything."

"Three pages."

"That's not fair."

"Another word and you've got detention."

I wrote *cocksucker* in my notebook.

I had the car that day, and after school I drove my friend Virginia and her boyfriend, Bobby, to Virginia's house. We ate Mystic Mint cookies and drank Cokes in her kitchen. I kept sighing, and V kept saying, "Poor Bev. I'm glad I'm not you." When I got up to leave, Bobby dove onto the floor, hugged his stomach, and rolled around laughing until tears fell down his cheeks. When he caught his breath, he said, "Your father's going to kill you." Bobby should know. His father was as much of a maniac as mine, only a Baptist. I walked out the door as though to an execution.

It was a half hour before dinnertime, and my parents were waiting for me at the table. I dropped my books and slumped into a chair. My mother stood up, leaned against the stove, and crossed her arms against her chest. "Well, I hope you're proud of yourself now," she said.

"No," I said.

"What are you going to do?"

"Marry Raymond."

"It's that easy. You're so smart. You know everything." She always said that. Probably because, since the seventh grade, I'd been rolling my eyes at everything she said and constantly correcting her grammar.

"No I don't."

My father was leafing through the pages of my notebook.

"And what about your boyfriend? What does he think about all this?"

"He's very happy. We're getting married."

My father tore a handful of pages from my notebook and threw them in front of my mother. On the table lay the pictures I drew in English class that day of balls and cocks erect and coming, with the words *suck, fuck, cocksucker, motherfucker* written in block letters and shaded like titles on a book. "Look, look what your daughter thinks about in school."

I ran out of the kitchen, past my sisters in the living room watching the *Mike Douglas Show*, and thought, Thank God my brother's not around to hear this—he was in the middle of the ocean somewhere, in the navy. I sat on the top step of the stairs to my room, pinched my face between my knees, and listened to my parents yell at each other in the kitchen.

"I knew it. I knew it. Trust her, you say. Leave the kid alone? So help me God, Grace, don't you ever tell me to trust those other two daughters of yours."

"Oh no, Sonny, you're not blaming me for this. She's your daughter too."

"What did I tell you she was doing in the cellar with her boyfriend? What did I tell you?"

All I could think about was Mindy Harmon. Mindy wasn't bad like me. Mindy was a cheerleader, never wore makeup, got drunk only rarely, didn't smoke cigarettes, and still she got pregnant. Her mother dragged her to all the basketball games where she was supposed to be cheerleading, just to shame her. Mindy was pathetic. She had to sit sideways at her desk, and she wore her skirts with the zipper open and the waist fastened with the three-inch safety pin she got from her cheerleading kilt. But whenever anybody asked her if she was pregnant, she'd blink her eyes twice and say no. I'd already told half the town about my condition. I might be pregnant, but I'd rather die than act ashamed like Mindy Harmon.

"Rose," my mother called. "Go tell your sister to get back here."

My nine-year-old sister stood at the bottom of the stairs and looked up at me. "Bev?" she whispered.

I was embarrassed to meet her eyes. She looked like she might start bawling. What was I doing, banished to the stairs like a scarlet woman? What kind of an example was I setting for my sisters? You'd think I'd murdered somebody the way my parents were acting, when all I did was have sexual intercourse—and not even that often.

My father was sobbing into his hands and my mother was picking crud from the crack down the middle of the table with a bobby pin when I sat back down and dug my heels in.

"You're killing your father," my mother said.

I shrugged my shoulders.

"Your father and I think you should give the baby up for adoption."

"No." I'd already made up my mind about that.

"Then keep it and live at home."

"No!" She had to be out of her mind. The one and only good thing about having a baby was that it would get me out of my parents' house.

My father blew his nose.

"Your father and I have discussed this. If you want, we'll adopt it. You're too young to get married. You'll regret it the rest of your life."

"Adopt it?" I stood up shouting. "You just want to steal my baby. I'm keeping it. I'm getting married. It's *my* baby."

"All right. All right." My father wasn't crying anymore. "You just calm down. You're underage, smart ass. You need our permission."

"I'll elope."

"You think it's fun? You think it's easy? You think that boyfriend of yours will be a good provider? You think he can keep a job and support you and a baby?"

"Mom was pregnant when you got married." This was my ace in the hole. I'd figured it out by subtraction, years ago. This was the first time I'd mentioned it.

"That was different," my mother said. "We were older. We knew what we were doing."

"Daddy was unemployed. You didn't have any money. You told me yourself. You lived in a shack."

"That's enough." My father stood up.

At the risk of getting slapped, I said one more thing after my father told me enough. "All I'm saying is it worked for you."

"All right. I give up. She knows everything." My father smacked the back of his chair. "I'm telling you, Beverly. You better be good and goddamn sure, because once you leave this house, you mark my words, you can't come back. You made your bed, you sleep in it."

I stared at the floor.

"Go to your room," he said.

I ran to my room, threw myself on the bed, and sobbed my heart out in spite of myself.

CHAPTER 3

THE weeping segued to the eve of my wedding. Ray was off at his bachelor party and I was sitting in Fay's kitchen with her mother and her mother's friend Joyce the manhater. They were drinking gin and Fay and I were drinking coffee. Joyce, who was a staple at Fay's house, was a vociferous opponent of marriage and a devout deballer of men. She liked nothing better than to drink her second martini and hold me and Fay captive with her invectives and warnings: "They're all big babies. You're better off alone, doing for yourself. Who needs them sniveling and complaining and pawing at you." Mr. Johnston walked in and poured himself a scotch, and Joyce went on like he wasn't there: "There's not a woman in the world that doesn't regret getting married. But they'd rather choke than admit it. I bet your mother just loves being married to a guinea. [Joyce and Fay's mother were Italian, too.] Does he slap her around if his meatballs are overdone?"

I liked that Fay's mother had a friend like Joyce. Fay's mother came from the Bronx and wore gaudy plastic jewelry and bright red lipstick and smoked cigarettes in an ivory cigarette holder. She let us smoke and swear in her house. One time she came home from work with a migraine in the middle of the day and found five of us playing hookey and dressed up in her clothes. She didn't say one word except, "I'm sick. I'm going to bed." This night she hardly said a word to me either. I thought she didn't like me anymore because I'd deserted to the enemy's camp. This made me very sad, and after my second piece of pie, I left Fay and her mother and Joyce to lie on the sofa in the living room, where Mr. Johnston sat doing the crossword puzzle under a lamp and sipping his scotch.

"So, Beverly," he said. "Big day tomorrow."

"Yeah."

"I thought you were going to be a great actress."

"I was."

"Well, you never know what might happen. I know what you need. What you need's a stage name, that'll perk you up."

I sat up. "Yeah?"

"I know, Viela, Viela Scaloppini, how's that? That's a good stage name for you."

Viela Scaloppini, I repeated the name to myself. It sounded familiar. It would stick in people's minds. "Hey, Fay," I called to the kitchen. "Your father made up a stage name for me, Viela Scaloppini."

"That's an Italian dish, Beverly," she said. "Veal and peppers or something."

Her father was laughing so hard the newspaper shook. I felt like bawling right there in front of him, but then I'd really seem a fool, so I waited until I went home shortly after, passed my sisters and parents watching TV in the living room, said good night to the floor and heard my mother say, "Got a big day tomorrow, don't stay up late," as I walked up the stairs to my room. I laid on top of my bed and thought, That's the last time my mother will say those words to me. This is the last time I'll sleep in my bed, the last time this will be my room. I looked around at the knotty-pine panels my father had hammered up one by one to make my brother, Mike, a bedroom. I'd moved in as soon as Mike left for the navy. I'd rearranged the furniture, but it had never really been my room anyway. I turned off the little lamp hanging by my bed. My mother had bought it on sale at Bradlees, where she worked in the candy and stationery department. It was bulbous and made of milk glass, with little lumps all over. Fay had said it was diseased and that the lumps looked like warts. I should have told her to shut up. I jammed a pillow over my face and cried myself to sleep.

It worked out for the best that Fay's father was a cruel man, because by the wedding ceremony the next morning I was all cried out, or maybe I was just so much of a contrary person that I was smiling because 90 percent of everybody else was crying. When I saw Fay and Beatrice, we broke into a giggling fit.

I avoided looking at Ray until he was five feet away. When I finally tried to meet his eyes, he was looking down at his hands. I remembered about his father. I looked in the front seat of Ray's side of the aisle. His mother and sister were leaning heads together weeping, and there was no sign of Ray's father, who had shown up in town fresh from the Bowery a couple of weeks before. We'd sent him an invitation, and then this morning Raymond was supposed to drop by his room with a red carnation in a see-through plastic box and bring him to the wedding.

At the altar, my father's eyes looked greener somehow. When he kissed me his cheek felt smooth as silk from shaving and slippery with tears. My mother looked beautiful in her new pink dress but she was practically convulsing with my two little sisters in the seat behind me, and then when Raymond came and took my hand, his mouth started trembling. I got annoyed because I wanted him to act like a man. But then when I took his hand and it was cold and shaking, I felt the way I did whenever I saw a midget or dwarf or a hunchbacked person—like I wanted to take them home and adopt them or something. So I covered his shaking hand with my hand, looked him in his eyes, and said, "I love you," even though a minute ago, at the top of the aisle, I wished he'd die before I turned thirty-five. The kid would be eighteen then, a legal adult, and I could start another life while I was still reasonably attractive.

By the time we'd reached Ray's sister's apartment in New York City for our honeymoon weekend, I was tired and grouchy and mad at Raymond for drinking shots of Seagram's 7 in the bar next to the hall, then for being found puking in the bathroom when it was time to cut the cake. I'd had my first drinks and cigarettes in front of my parents. I'd danced nearly every dance. I'd led the Bunny Hop and laughed and joked and passed out cookies. Now that it was over, I felt like a discarded flower. Ray's sister had left us a bottle of champagne in the refrigerator and two champagne glasses with our names engraved like frost across them. Ray and I linked arms and took a sip, then slunk into bed. After we fumbled around in the dark for a while, I remembered about Ray's father. "What happened to your dad?" I said.

"He didn't answer the door."

"You brought the flower and knocked and he didn't answer?"

Ray nodded his head.

"How do you know he was there?"

"I could hear cartoons on."

"Do you feel bad?"

"It would've been weird if he came."

"I wish I could meet him."

"No you don't."

I pulled Raymond's head to my chest. He put his hand on my belly. Dionne Warwick's "Do You Know the Way to San Jose?" came on the radio. It made me think of dancing with my father at the wedding. I'd looked forward to it for weeks. I pictured us doing the cha cha, the lindy, the fox-trot, a waltz, just like he'd danced with my mother for us kids in the kitchen Saturday nights when they were all dressed up and about to go out. I pictured the whole group of people down in the basement hall of the Italian Club stopping just to watch me gliding across the floor with my handsome father. But my father never asked me to dance again after the first one, when he gave me away. In bed with Raymond, I thought I should've been brave enough to ask him.

After the reception, everyone had gone to my house. Ray and I changed in my bedroom and counted our money. We had eight hundred dollars, which would pay for the hospital. Then we played the Four Tops in the basement with my cousins and friends for an hour or so before Bobby and Virginia drove us to the train. When Bobby peeled out of the driveway, I saw my father look out the window.

"There must be a dozen cops in that house," Virginia said.

"They ain't going to do nothing to me," said Bobby. "I'm going to Nam in a couple of months."

"A real hero." Virginia flipped her fall off her shoulder and looked out the window.

At the stop sign, when Bobby slammed on the brakes and peeled out again, Raymond said, "Hey, we got a pregnant girl here, man." I don't know why, but I'd felt like Raymond and Virginia were on one team and Bobby and I were on another.

"Put a dollar down and buy a car," Dionne's song brought me back to my honeymoon and future life— "In a week maybe two they'll make you a star"—and I felt the tears coming. Raymond put his head on my belly. "I think it's moving," he said.

CHAPTER 4

FOR most of my life my family and I lived in a little mint-green house that was officially part of the public-housing project but was perched on the very edge of it. Across our back lawn and down a field of weeds sat the rest of the publicly owned homes, tiny Cape Cods on minuscule plots of scorched grass or long brick apartment buildings set at strange angles to the street. Teenagers peeled out from stop sign to stop sign down there and kids ran around in huge stick-wielding packs. But across the road from our front lawn were big privately owned houses, fire-engine-red, snow-white, and forest green, with long lawns, generous trees, and kids who said please and thank you. At the very top of our hill was the country club.

Whenever I told anyone I lived on Long Hill, they assumed it was in one of the big houses and I didn't correct them. There'd been a time when I hung out at the project by a chain-link fence, French-inhaling cigarettes and flirting with boys who said *pussy* and *twat*. My best friend Donna broke up with me over my attraction to the project. But that was a long time ago, back during the fall when everyone at Dag Hammarskjold Junior High School mistook that plane for the Russians. Since then I'd come to think that most of the people from the project were two things: poor and weird. Like Susan Gerace and her father, Anthony, whose backyard I could see from my bedroom window. Anthony dressed up in his World War II uniform to play his bugle every chance he got—like on Memorial Day, at high school graduations, assemblies after assassinations, and every other evening after dinner. He stood with Susan in their backyard and made her play "Taps," too. If she got even one note wrong he slapped her on the ear and made her do it over until she got it right. Only then would Anthony answer her with his sad, clear high-pitched horn, putting her playing to shame no matter how perfect her notes. It seems that every night of my life I'd digested dinner to "Taps." For this I blamed my parents. I looked down on them for landing us in the project, for not owning their own home, for not graduating high school—so they could get good jobs and afford their own home—and for never having enough money for anything, like dancing lessons or enough expensive clothes.

So I took it as yet another kind of poetic justice, or should I say just punishment, that I ended up leaving school before I graduated and being grateful to my father for pulling some strings and jumping Raymond and me to the top of the public-housing-authority waiting list. We got an apartment in a peeling mint-green duplex house on a dead-end street called Backes Court, which, luckily, was separated from the rest of the project by about a mile. On the first floor we had a kitchen with an emerald-green floor, blue brick contact paper behind the stove, and a living room with a picture window. On the second floor were two small bedrooms, ours and Baby's, and a bathroom at the top of the stairs, with a Chiquita banana sticker on the doorknob. In our yard we had one dead bush and no trees.

On our new road, kids rumbled on Big Wheels all day, dug holes in yards, which they filled with water to make mud balls to throw at each other. The mothers shook blankets from upstairs windows and sat in the sun on front stoops, their hair rolled up and drying. The few remaining fathers drove off in cars and returned once a day, which was what Raymond did, while I plopped around the house like a fat tomato. Most of my time was spent at the window, watching and wishing I'd have the nerve to ask one of those women over for tea and cinnamon sticks or something—when I wasn't stuck doing schoolwork, that is.

It had been arranged for me to be tutored so I could graduate high school. That meant I had to invite every teacher I'd formerly sassed into my impoverished teenage home decorated in cast-off furniture that had made a detour to my house on its way to the dump. In other words, I ate crow as my teachers wiped their feet on my welcome mat and sat in my Flintstone furniture—old stuff that belonged to an aunt and had been reupholstered hard as rock. When I handed them my meticulously done homework assignments, not one of them, not even O'Rourke, who chain-smoked and smelled vaguely of booze, ever made a crack, which made me feel pitied instead of relieved. I never had to hear I told you so, but I did have to put up with my home economics teacher's conversation—like when Bobby Kennedy got shot and she objected to there being no day off from work like there'd been for Martin Luther King. She said it was "just because Martin Luther King's black." I figured that was a good enough reason, when you considered how many black leaders we had in the country, but I kept my mouth shut because she was the teacher and I was the pregnant teenager making a pink dress with five seams so I could let one out every time my stomach grew another inch.

Then came graduation, which I couldn't attend because of my big belly, not to mention that I wasn't invited. My friends called me the next day to give me the details. They told me the principal had stood at the podium after handing out the diplomas and said, "And congratulations to Beverly Donofrio, who couldn't join us today." My friends swore to me that nobody, not one person, snickered or yelled out a joke, and I was so grateful, I felt love for every single classmate I had formerly called a jerk or moron or imbecile.

I wasn't so in love with my friends, though, because they'd deserted me to go have the best time of their lives at a cottage they'd rented by a lake an hour away. So all summer long my main companions besides Raymond were Bam Bam, a retarded three-year-old, and my mother, who stopped by every morning and every afternoon too, since my house was on her way to everywhere and since she figured I was lonely and needed her.

One morning she came in the back door and called, "Yooo hooo."

I was still in bed. It was ten-thirty.

"You up?"

"Yeah."

I heard her banging around in the kitchen, and pulled on my jeans with the stretchy stomach pouch, which my mother had bought me on one of our afternoon jaunts to Barkers, Stars, or Caldor. I padded down the stairs and into the kitchen.

"It's gonna be a scorcher," she said, placing two coffee cups on the table.

"I don't want any."

"What do you want, juice?"

I nodded.

"I brought you some leftover stew." She pointed to a plastic container in the refrigerator. "And there's some of those stuffed peppers, too."

"They give me heartburn."

"That's one thing I never got. But I held my water, especially with you. My legs swelled up like balloons. And the poison ivy that year? I thought I'd die. Ray likes peppers. Warm them up for him."

She sat down, lit another cigarette, and took a sip of coffee. "When'd you do the wash last?"

The last time I did the wash was when she'd done it. "I don't know," I said.

"You got to keep on top of it. Do you want to do a load now?"

"No, Ma, it's too hot." She was beginning to piss me off.

"You can do it tonight, you know. I used to do that. Once it cools down, throw a load in, then hang them out, they'll be dry before noon."

"I'm so bored I can't stand it."

"It's not like you don't have plenty to do—you just don't do it. When did you mop the floor last?"

"I don't want to talk about housework."

"I'm just telling you for your own good. You get into a routine, then it's easy."

"Ma!" I yelled. "I don't want to talk about housework, okay?" She got up and started sponging off the counters. I looked at the clock. I still had an hour before my first soap opera.

"Tell me how you and Daddy met." I said it to change the subject and keep her around, even though I'd heard the story a hundred times, like I'd heard all her stories a hundred times—because I'd been her main confidante since the day I was born, only back then she was fun. She used to sing in the kitchen, tap-dance down the hallway, and sometimes do back bends on the lawn.

She sat down and lit another cigarette. "We were at a dance at Rockaway Park. All the big bands came there. Your father was with his buddies and they were teasing him in front of me, saying, 'Why don't you jitterbug with Grace?' He wasn't asking me because he had the piles and they knew it."

"He couldn't dance because he had piles?"

"Well, you know, they were uncomfortable. He was shy. The next Saturday I asked him to dance. You know your father, he's a good dancer. And then we started dating, and six months later we married." I figured my mother must've been a hot number because she didn't hold sex off very long. "My family disowned me. They never liked Daddy, said he was a bum. I don't think your father ever forgot that."

"Do you wish you never got married?"

"Oh, you know. When I was single, I had a job, I had money, I bought nice clothes, went on vacations. I did what I pleased. Then when you marry, you go where the man wants. I moved to Wallingford. I hated it. I didn't know nobody. Then you kids came. I don't know. If you want to be happy, you stay single."

"But you love Daddy?"

"Oh yeah. But I cried in the beginning. I was so homesick. I missed my friends. I missed my job. And your father never wanted me to work. A man has his pride. But once I got my license—you were, what were you, fifteen?—I said, the hell with this. We needed money. That's when I started down Bradlees. Now, my legs, standing on those concrete floors. And taking care of two houses. I'm not getting any younger, you know." My mother could only talk for so long before she started complaining.

"Ma, you don't have to clean my house." I tried to nip it in the bud.

"Yeah, well, once you have the baby, I won't, believe me." Just then Bam Bam knocked on the door with his head. Bam Bam never said a word except "Bam Bam" and he only said that when he knocked on your door with his head.

"Are you going to let him in?" my mother said.

"Yes." I got up and opened the door.

"What you let him in for?"

"I like him."

Bam Bam sat at the table between us.

"Honest to God, Beverly, I can't believe you're having a baby in a couple of months. You better grow up." This was her favorite and most irritating thing to say. "Have you met any neighbors yet?"

"No."

She raised her eyebrows.

I should want to talk to Bam Bam's aunt—the woman he and his sisters lived with? She ignored her children, looked like a walrus, and lived with a guy who had no teeth. Or the lady across the street, who polished her red GTO as often as she changed her clothes? It was true sometimes I wished I could invite one or two of the prettier ones over, but the one time I did talk to neighbors it had been a big mistake. They were Stu and Marsha Heckle, who lived on the other side of my house. I called them the Uglies because he had big angry pimples and a pin head while she was shaped like a mushroom and you could see her pink scalp through her hair. As if being so ugly weren't enough, they were also Jehovah's Witnesses. I was sitting on the front steps, while Raymond watched a

baseball game inside, and Mr. Ugly came out and offered me a brownie "the Mrs." had made for a meeting
they were having that night of the Parents Against Sex
Education in Schools Committee. "You really think
sex education's wrong?" I ventured.

"Darned right," said Mr. Ugly. "Some stranger
telling our kids about the birds and the bees? What
gives them the right to take prayers out of the class-
room and replace them with sex?"

This made me want to barf, since I figured if somebody had given me the scoop on birth control, I might
not be stuck, a pregnant teenager on a front stoop in
the public-housing project listening to a perverted
Christian confuse prayers and sex.

"Like the Uglies?" I said to my mother. "I'm supposed to talk to people who don't believe in sex education?"

"Everybody's entitled to their opinions."

"And so am I. I *like* Bam Bam. And I wish you'd
butt out. It's my business who I talk to."

"I better go."

I immediately felt bad for yelling. "What're you
cooking tonight?"

"I don't know. It's so hot, I thought I'd just have
kielbasa and potato salad. And you?"

"Sloppy joes."

"Why don't you have the stew? I don't know how
you kids can eat that stuff."

"Ma."

"All right, all right. I got to go pick up a few
things at Jeannie's. You want to come, you need anything?" Jeannie's was my father's cousin Jeannie's
store, and every time I went there, she threw a box of
goodies in my bag, like Ring Dings or Drake's Coffee
Cakes or a gallon of ice cream.

"No," I said.

She opened the refrigerator and lifted the quart of milk. "You need more milk." She opened the freezer. "That was the last can of juice? I'll pick some up."

She washed the cups and left.

I turned on the TV and watched my soaps with Bam Bam; then at around five I told the Bammer to go home for dinner. I opened up a can of sloppy-joe mix, put two hamburger buns on each of our plates, and warmed some Green Giant corn. Sometimes Ray and I sat in front of the TV and ate off snack trays, but tonight I thought we'd sit on the back stoop, where it was cooler.

When Ray hadn't shown up by five-thirty, I sat on the stoop with my plate balanced on my knees and tried not to get too worried. The first few times Ray was late I let my imagination run away, picturing him in his car wrapped around a tree or swallowed by a machine at work or simply driving and driving away from me and out of sight. But this time I figured he was probably just getting shitfaced as usual in a bar with some guy from work I'd never met.

After I finished dinner, I switched to the front stoop to watch for Ray's car. I hoped Bam Bam and Berta and Betty, his two beautiful five- and six-year-old sisters, would show. Berta and Betty had bright red hair and startling blue eyes, but they were always filthy dirty and ragged just like their little brother. I almost felt as sorry for Berta and Betty as I did for Bam Bam, because sometimes I'd look out at night and there the two of them would be—their curly heads in the dark—walking in the gutter, Berta in front, Betty in back, just walking up and down the street looking at their feet.

They came running from their yard when they saw

me. Bam Bam sat up close as I directed Berta and Betty in acrobatics. They did cartwheels around the rim of my yard, then crisscrossed each other in a big X, doing back flips. They did the routine over and over until they got the timing right and wound up in front of me at exactly the same moment. Then I taught them to curtsy, their arms curved like the necks of swans. I swear, the two of them would've made it to the Olympics if their aunt would only push them.

It was just getting dark when Berta and Betty's aunt stood on her back stoop and called, "Beeertaaa, Beeetteeey." If she looked my way, she would've seen them, but she didn't. Just stood on her stoop, round like an apple, with her hands cupped to her mouth, then went back in the house. Berta and Betty stopped dead in their tracks. The screen door slammed like a gunshot. They took off and didn't look back. They never said goodbye.

I heard Bam Bam rustling under the bush and making that whiny noise he did. I'd lost track of him, and now his knees were caked with dirt and there was snot dried on his face. "Crying out loud, Bam Bam," I said. "Doesn't your aunt ever wash you?" He smiled a slit smile and wagged his head back and forth real fast. "Want me to wash your face for you, Bammerang?" He kept shaking his head back and forth. I took a rag and loaded it with suds then washed his face like I was polishing a car. He squirmed around and squealed. It's not that I was a nut for cleanliness. That was my mother. I think it was more that Bam Bam was the type of kid people naturally liked to torture—like the neighborhood psychopath, Andrew, who could chase Bam Bam with a willow whip for hours.

Bam Bam pointed at the refrigerator, turned his palms up next to his shoulders, then shrugged them to his ears. He had some cute ways about him. You know how they say retarded people are closer to God? I believed that about Bam Bam. He didn't have a mean bone in his body, and his life was pretty grim. I think his aunt wished he'd just disappear, get kidnapped or run over by a truck or something. You never heard her calling, "Berta, Betty, Bam Bam."

It was late, near nine o'clock, and I was trying hard to keep my mind off of Raymond so I wouldn't get furious. I got Bam Bam a Ring Ding Jr. and poured him a glass of strawberry Kool-Aid, then I sat at the table across from him with my Ring Ding and glass of Kool-Aid and he did like Simon Says. He peeled the wrapper exactly like me, then held the round chocolate thing with his pointer finger and thumb the same as me. Then I licked under it to be sure it wasn't my imagination, and he licked it too. Bam Bam cracked me up.

It was pitch-black out; a breeze was kicking up and whipping the shades against the windows. I was spooked and glad Bam Bam was there. "Hey, Bam," I said. "You want to dance?" He nodded his head up and down fast. I put *Sgt. Pepper* on the stereo. I was careful not to lift my arms up high because my mother was always warning me that I'd strangle the baby with the umbilical cord. So I twirled and swayed my gigantic hips and Bam Bam did little hops and wiggled his head.

I collapsed exhausted and sweaty in the rocker.

Bam Bam tried to climb on my lap.

I didn't want him to touch me. "Get off," I said.

He made like he'd start crying.

"Don't you cry, Bammer, or I won't let you in anymore. Hear me? You better go now." I opened the front door. He just stood there. "Bam Bam," I said with forced patience.

He bent his chin to his chest and crouched down like an ape. When he finally passed through, I locked the door and headed upstairs. He banged his head on the screen, "Bam . . . bam, bam . . . bam," he said.

I screamed, "Bam Bam, get lost. I mean it!"

I ran up the stairs and sat on the edge of our bed and stared out the window in the dark. I spotted Bam Bam sitting in the gutter a few feet down the road, swishing sand with a stick and rubbing his eye with the back of his hand. I felt bad kicking him out, but I didn't want to call him back, either.

Just then a car approached in a whoosh of light and I thought maybe it was my mother. It was Raymond. He slammed the door a little too hard.

His feet made a lot of noise on the floor. He called, "Beverly."

I didn't answer.

"Fuck," he said.

He opened the refrigerator door and closed it. I heard the water go on. He walked up the stairs, took a piss in the bathroom. I held my breath. He looked in the room and said, "What're you doing?"

"You should have called."

He leaned against the door frame. He smelled of cigarettes and booze. "That guy, Sal? Got laid off. He didn't expect it, either. Some of us guys went down the Aviation for some drinks to make him feel better."

I laid down on my stomach and started to cry.

"What's the matter?" he said.

"I don't know," I lied. The matter was I wanted my mother.

I had big plans for my marriage. They went something like this: My friends come over every night. We have pajama parties and play music as loud as we want. Instead, like I said, they deserted me to Spring Lake, where they had new and changing boyfriends, went skinny-dipping and floating on inner tubes, and never thought of inviting me, because I was pregnant. The only girlfriends who called me up were Virginia, who would be going to college in the fall and had to stay in Wallingford to work for the summer, and Fay, because she was married now too. She'd married the guy from the nuclear submarine the day after graduation, as planned.

Finally, my friends invited us to a huge party. Ray and I drove Virginia and Bobby, who would be leaving for boot camp in a couple of weeks. Everybody would be there except for Fay, because she was visiting her in-laws in Virginia. By the time of the party, it had been positively confirmed that Fay had conceived on her honeymoon. I was ecstatic that now I wouldn't be the only mother.

I could think of nothing but the party for weeks. I was sure everybody would be shocked to see how fat I'd grown and that they'd make a big fuss over me. But my girlfriends seemed different. For one thing, their skin was tanned, and for another, they were surrounded by guys I'd never laid eyes on. There were empty beer cans and scotch bottles overflowing from garbage bags in corners. Beatrice, who used to think she was ugly, was wearing tight hiphuggers and a low-cut jersey. She was with a guy named Donnie, who'd just come back from Vietnam, where he'd been a paramedic. But his last three months all he did was load bodies in plastic bags onto planes. Beatrice told me this in the bathroom while she plucked her eyebrows. "I'm such a mess, Beverly. I've been drunk for a month."

"Really?"

"We have beer for breakfast. Beer and toast."

"You're lucky."

"I'm broke. I spent all my graduation money. We all are. In two weeks I start at the Knights of Columbus with my mother. I don't want to go back to Wallingford. You're lucky you don't have to work."

"I know."

No one made a fuss about my hugeness, so after my third rum and Coke, I lifted my shirt up in the kitchen to show off my belly. People gathered around to touch it. "What does it feel like?" they wanted to know.

"Heavy. I get backaches and heartburn."

"Ugh."

"But it moves. Sometimes you can see it under my skin."

"How weird."

Then I got drunk, noticed this beautiful guy walk in the door, and forgot myself. I asked him to dance. We did the Jerk and I forgot all about the umbilical cord and fetus strangulation and that I was even pregnant. I closed my eyes and really got into it. I imagined he was watching me and wishing I wasn't married. I imagined that if I weren't married, I would dance with this guy for the rest of the night. Then we'd go outside and talk by the lake. He'd be from a different town. We'd go there and I'd meet new people. I felt his hand on my arm and opened my eyes. "Won't you hurt the baby?" he said.

I turned and walked through the kitchen and out the back door, stunned. I sat on the ground between two parked cars until I was sure I wouldn't cry, then I looked for Raymond. He was leaning against a car. He took the last swig of a beer, then squashed the can in his fist and burped. He was with Armond White, who was home on leave from the army.

"You're drunk," I said when I stood next to Raymond.

"Tell me one thing," Ray said. "We were just talking. How do you lose my socks in the wash? What the hell happens to them?"

"You've had too much to drink," I said.

"Ah, come on."

"I want to go home."

"We just got here."

"Why don't you leave the guy alone?" Armond said. I had a longstanding gripe with Armond. He was the moron who told Raymond that if you had sex more than once in twenty-four hours then you were safe after the first time. I knew Armond was stupid, like most of Raymond's friends, but I believed him because I thought they taught guys all about birth control in the army.

"Mind your own business, Armond," I said.

"You let your wife talk like that, man?"

"*Let* your wife? I talk however the fuck I please."

"Nice language."

"Raymond." I thought I'd murder him if he didn't walk away with me that instant.

"You think you're pretty tough, huh?" said Armond. "Remember, tough cookies crumble."

"All over your face."

"Beverly, come on." Raymond hugged me from behind and pinned my arms to my sides as he walked me away backward.

"You have such assholes for friends," I said.

"So? I'm an asshole," Ray said.

"Let's go home."

"I'm having fun. We never have fun anymore. Don't let's leave yet. Please? Besides, what about Bobby and Virginia?"

"How can you even talk to somebody so stupid? I'm so tired."

"You're always tired. You hate my friends. We never have any fun." He tried to kiss me on the neck. "Come on, Bevy. All your friends are here. You been looking forward to this for weeks. Why aren't you having fun?"

"If we stay longer you'll get drunker."

"I promise. If we stay another two hours, I won't drink anymore. Maybe one beer."

"One hour."

"All right."

One hour later I couldn't find him. An hour after that, I found him lying on his back on top of a picnic table by the lake. Drunk. I told him I wanted to go home.

"I want to go home. I want to go home. You know who you sound like? What's her name in *The Wizard of Oz*." He thought that was a riot.

"You said only one beer."

He sat up and swayed so far to the right he almost fell off the table. I felt like hitting him. "Give me the keys," I said.

He dug in his pockets, then shook his head up from his chest. "What am I doing? No way. You're really something." He pointed his thumb at me. "The big boss. Everybody thinks I'm pussy-whipped. That's why I got drunk."

"I'm going," I said, and started walking toward home, which was fifty miles away. The road was dark and deserted. I passed the little stand, closed now, where the year before I'd sat on a picnic table and flirted with some college guys who'd asked me if I was a nonconformist, a word I'd never heard. I'd walked nearly a mile and was not only getting cold but scared, because the trees made an arch over my head and blocked off the moonlight, when Raymond finally pulled up with Virginia and Bobby in the backseat. "You walked far," he said.

"I'm freezing," I said.

"Get in, baby," he said.

"Let me drive."

"Please, Bev?"

I felt sorry for him. I could be a bitch. Plus, I didn't want to make a scene in front of Virginia and Bobby, who'd seen too many already, so I got in and ignored his weaving all over the road. About ten minutes later, Raymond nodded out and our VW flipped like a pancake. Sand chimed around me and time slowed down as I thought, Now, at last, I'll lose the baby.

Then everything was still and silent. Virginia said, "Bobby?"

"I'm all right," he said.

"Beverly?" she said.

"I'm okay," I said as I squeezed myself out of the upside-down car. Bobby and Virginia looked dazed standing a foot apart staring. The only sound was the whir of wheels spinning. "Where's Ray?" Bobby said after a minute. It was strange we'd forgotten him.

We walked like zombies to the other side of the car. Raymond was lying on the ground, unconscious, with the car door resting on his shoulder and a big blob of blood gelling on the asphalt under his nose.

"Do you think it's his brain?" I said.

Bobby put his ear to Ray's chest. "He's alive," he said.

We walked across the street and banged on a door. A woman's voice yelled, "Get out of here before I call the cops."

Bobby said, "Fuck you, lady."

At the next house, the woman called an ambulance and we went back to the car to wait.

"Goddamn!" Bobby kicked a fender.

"Bobby, don't," Virginia said, because Bobby could get crazy.

"That's my buddy," Bobby said. "Look at him, man."

I couldn't. Neither could Virginia.

At the hospital they wheeled Ray away, then a doctor examined me. He listened to my stomach with a stethoscope and said the baby seemed fine. Then he bandaged my knee and my forehead where it had hit the windshield and told me I could go home. Bobby and Virginia got picked up by Virginia's father, and I hung around to wait for Ray to get out of X rays. His eyes were black-and-blue and opened. When he saw me, he started crying.

"His collarbone and his nose are broken," a nurse told me.

"I should've let you drive," Raymond cried.

"It's all right," I said.

"I could've killed you. I love you so much."

"I love you too. Don't cry."

The nurse rolled him away sobbing.

"You all right?" my father said when I called home for a ride. I'd been praying I'd get my mother.

"Yes."

"Him?"

"Broken collarbone and nose."

"Was he drinking?"

"A little."

"Did they book him?"

"No."

"The car?"

"Totaled."

"Jesus Christ. What's the matter with you kids? I ought to have his license taken away. Now, what're you gonna do for a car?"

My mother came to pick me up, then it was her turn. "He's gonna miss work," she said. "What're you going to do for money? I do what I can, but you know your father and me don't have a pot to piss in. I don't know, you kids think you can go around acting like teenagers."

"We are teenagers."

"You're having a baby. You have responsibilities. What's it going to be like when the baby's born? How would you've felt if you lost it? You better smarten up."

I leaned my head back on the seat and watched the streetlights disappear into the car roof and hummed not a song but a drone, like a bumble bee.

"What's that?" my mother said.

I kept humming, and she never knew it was me.

Once I got home, I was afraid murderers and escapees from mental institutions were lurking by the windows, so I went directly to the bathroom, locked the door, and sat on the floor next to the toilet. I felt so lonely, I even confessed to myself that I wished I could've gone home with my mother. I hugged the bowl and yowled great sobs like opera.

Then the baby moved. It was the first time since the accident. My crying trembled to neutral.

Maybe I'd been lonely for the baby. I realized I'd been talking to her for months without thinking. Maybe I would've been sad if she died.

I went to a fortune-teller by the railroad tracks. Her trailer smelled of cat piss, and she was as wide as a Volkswagen. She sat me down and dealt some cards.

She said I was having a girl, which I already knew, and that within five years I'd have two more children and move into a split-level house. My daughter's name would begin with *J*.

I began making plans. My daughter would look just like me, and when she was born she'd have a round little baseball head covered with black hair. Her eyes would be big and brown. She was going to be my best friend and there'd be nothing in the world we wouldn't talk about. I'd tell her every last detail about my life up to her birth and after. She'd definitely go to college, and I'd call her Nicole, after a schizophrenic on my favorite soap opera. Ray said if it was a boy, he wanted it named after him. I said, no way. I wasn't naming our girl after me. We settled on Jason, after Jason McCord in *The Lawman,* and his middle name would be Michael, after my father.

CHAPTER 5

LABOR started on a Sunday night in the middle of September. It was so hot that week that the neighborhood dogs had taken to roaming in packs in a flurry of heat madness. Cats dived under cars and into open cellar windows to escape them. One day I saw the dogs toss a doll in the air and rip it limb from limb, a cloud of white foam clinging to their coats. I was almost two weeks late, and if I didn't deliver soon, I was planning to throw myself in the middle of that pack of mangy dogs and be done for.

We went for macaroni at my mother's on Sunday, a ritual I'd missed maybe a half dozen times in my entire life, only this time I felt a pain after dinner while we were watching *The FBI* and eating lemon meringue pie, but I didn't say anything. Raymond wanted to stay for the Sunday night movie, but I told him I didn't feel too well and wanted to go home. As soon as we walked into our house, a slimy liquid drooled down the inside of my thigh. "Oooh, gross! Raymond!" I yelled. "I think I'm in labor."

"You're kidding," he said.

We tossed my overnight bag into the backseat of our Chevelle (my father had found it for five hundred dollars and co-signed for the loan), and I suggested we take a ride once around the duck pond before we went to the hospital. The new Beatles song "Hey Jude" came on the radio.

"That's it!" I said. "That's what we'll name her— June." I'd misheard the lyrics.

Ray drummed his thumbs on the dashboard, jerked his chin in and out, and said, "Cool."

I was scared to death in the labor room. First they shaved me, then they gave me an enema, then after I waddled out of the bathroom and back into the room, they laid me in a crib like a beached whale. Immediately, the nurse poked some fingers in. I was three fingers, the middle circle. Five fingers was the biggest. When you stretched that wide it was bingo, birth. The Puerto Rican women came in and left within half an hour, screaming, *"Mama! Mama! Mama!"*

There was a pretty woman lying in the crib across from me. "Hi," she said after the nurse left.

"Hi."

"I'm Louise Baker. This is my first baby. You too?"

"Yeah. My name's Beverly Bouchard."

"If I scream like those ladies, shoot me, okay?"

"You think it's gonna really hurt?"

"I'm sure it does, but it can't hurt that much."

"How long you been here?"

"About an hour. I haven't seen a doctor yet. I go to the clinic."

"So do I. I never saw you."

"That place is the pits." She pulled back her long blond hair and began making a braid. "I go to Central Connecticut College. I mean, I did. After I was six months, I quit. My boyfriend still goes there. I'll probably go back after the baby."

"What were you going to school for?"

"My major? Anthropology."

I wasn't sure I knew what that was, but I'd rather die than ask her. I noticed her legs weren't shaved. I wished I'd seen her at the clinic. Everybody else spoke Spanish, and there never were enough folding chairs to go around. I'd had to wait a minimum of four hours every time, and if I'd met Louise there, we could've talked for whole mornings. By now we'd be good friends. But, probably, a person who went to college would think I was too stupid.

"Do you have medical insurance?" she asked.

"No. You?"

"Do you realize if you don't marry, your boy-friend's insurance won't cover you? We refused to marry. We put our politics in action. Art and I believe it's an archaic formality binding you together by law. My parents don't even . . . oh boy. Here comes one."

My pains had stopped altogether. I told the nurse. A doctor came in. He was young and handsome. His hands were slender and long. I'd never laid eyes on him before. "Hello," he said. He looked at my chart. "Mrs. Bouchard, I hear your pains have stopped."

"Yes."

"We're going to give you a little something to get them started again, speed things up."

The nurse handed him a needle and he stuck it in my ass. Within ten minutes, I was in agony and there was no breather between contractions. The doctor came back and said, "Okay, Mrs. Bouchard, we're moving right along. Now, I'm going to give you some Demerol to ease it up a bit." He gave me another shot in the ass. Before I passed out, I had a hallucination. I saw the kitten I'd had when I was a kid. It was jump-ing up over and over again, trying to get in the crib with me.

I don't know how long I was out before I awoke to Louise screaming, "Oh God, oh God, oh God. Ah ah ah ah *aaaahhhhhh!*"

Sweat started raining from every pore of my body. When she stopped screaming, she saw me looking at her through the bars and said, "I'm sorry, but it hurts so much," then she started crying.

I wished I could die.

Louise was long gone when the nurse rolled me onto my back, put my ankles in my hands, and told me to push. It was too humiliating. I kept thinking how even Jacqueline Kennedy must've held her ankles in the air and grunted like she was taking a shit. The next time the nurse appeared, she looked between my legs and started breathing heavily. "Okay, Mrs. Bouchard, I'd like you to stop pushing now. We're paging your doctor. Don't worry, everything's fine."

"I can't help it," I cried. "I have to."

"Please, Mrs. Bouchard, try not to push," she said as she wheeled my cot into the delivery room. I felt betrayed by every living mother. Why hadn't they warned me?

"This is horrible." I started crying. "Where's the gas? Give me the gas," I yelled. "Don't I get gas?" The nurse strapped my knees into stirrups, then positioned a round mirror above to distract me. "Look, Mrs. Bouchard, look. You can see the head." It was slimy green and protruding. I covered my eyes and yelled, "Take it away, I can't stand it, I don't want to!" Finally, an Oriental intern walked in. They clamped a gas mask on my face and it was over.

When I awoke, the nurse held a wrinkled, ugly red baby in a white cloth out to me. "Congratulations, Mrs. Bouchard, you have a healthy eight-and-a-half-pound baby boy."

"Boy!" I screamed. His head was huge and shaped like a football. "What's the matter with his head? He has blond hair!" The nurse blanched. I covered my face with my hands and sobbed. It was as though my daughter had died. The baby girl with the pretty round head who'd been hiccupping, rolling over, and kicking inside me—the daughter who'd been my best friend for months—had been a boy all along. What would I do with him? I didn't even like boys anymore. He'd have army men and squirt guns and baseball cards and a *penis*. What would we talk about?

My mother brought me a strawberry milkshake and kissed me on the cheek, then sat down and settled her pocketbook on her lap. "So, how does it feel to be a mother?" she asked.

I shrugged.

"Hurt, huh?"

I bit my lips to keep from crying.

Later, I took a walk to the nursery and saw him, a little lump under a white blanket. I thought if it weren't for his name on the bassinet, I wouldn't even know he was mine.

My mother came back at the next visiting hour and brought my father and my sisters, Rose and Phyllis, with her. Ray's mother came too, and so did three of my girlfriends. Everybody sat on my bed or the windowsills. Rose sat on my father's lap. When Ray came by after work, there was no place for him. He seemed like an outsider, and I felt sorry. He handed me a bunny with an ivy plant in its back, and the first opening he got, he rocked forward and back and said, "Hey, Bev, you know something? The song's 'Hey Jude,' not 'June.'"

Since the Beatles had been singing about a boy all along, maybe having a boy wouldn't be too bad. Besides, if the fortune-teller had been wrong about the sex of my baby, then she was probably wrong about the other two kids and the split-level house, too. "Do you think we should name him Jude instead of Jason?" I asked Ray.

"I guess."

"Jude?" my mother said. "What kind of a name's that?"

I'd never heard of St. Jude or *Jude the Obscure,* and the name reminded me of Judas, Jesus' traitor. I changed my mind. "Let's call him Jason," I said.

"Cool." Ray dragged on his cigarette.

The next day, when Jason came to my room, he was soft and warm and smelled sweet like baby, but he moved his head like a dinosaur in a Japanese movie. I was scared of him. Then he got the hiccups after half an ounce of milk and started crying.

He was still crying when I gave him back to the nurse. "Only half an ounce?" she said.

"He got the hiccups," I explained.

She shook her head as if to say, Stupid teenage mother.

The next time he came to my room, I made myself be braver. I shut the door, then took off his undershirt and memorized exactly how his diaper was pinned so I could duplicate it, then took it off too. I'd never seen an uncircumsised penis before. It looked like an elephant's trunk. I kissed it. I nuzzled his stomach, his armpit, his neck. I put his whole foot in my mouth.

The day we left the hospital, I dressed Jason in a blue suit with a plastic Tweety Bird glued on the chest. Ray carried him to the car like he was a tank of nitroglycerin. At a traffic light, when I noticed his head being led around by his mouth, I stuck my finger in. He sucked on it.

My mother was at our house when we got there and it looked like she'd been there for weeks. For one thing, it was spic-and-span, and for another, she'd moved the kitchen table from kitty-corner to flush against the wall. She was sitting at it with a tray of pastries and a pot of coffee in front of her. "You have more room this way," she said. I sat down and said, "Ma, look." I stuck my finger in.

"Take that finger out of his mouth! Are you crazy?" she said.

"Why? He likes it."

"You got germs on your hands. Everything that passes that baby's lips has to be sterilized. Come on, Jason." She held out her arms. I handed him over. "How you doin', little fella? What a big boy you are." She pinched his cheeks. "How you doing? How you doing? How you doing?" she shouted at him, nodding her head every time, poking his chin with her finger. "Look at those fat cheeks. I could eat him up. Your mother's tired, so your Mimi's taking over, let her get her strength back. Isn't that right?"

"Your *Mimi*?"

"It's cute, don't you think?"

"I like it," Ray said, taking off his jacket and sitting on the couch.

"Raymond, hang it up," my mother said. "Your wife just had a baby, she can't be picking up after you."

"I think Mimi's stupid."

"What's the matter with it?"

"It sounds like a dog."

"I like it. It'll be easier to pronounce."

I figured either she wanted to be called Mimi because she was only forty-five and embarrassed to be a grandmother or because Mimi sounded more like Mommy than Grandma did.

My mother came over for hours every single day. I hardly had to do anything, and when I did do something, she watched me like a hawk. "Watch out for his head, Beverly, don't forget the soft spot. His neck isn't strong yet, he could snap it. . . . Better put him on his stomach, he might spit up and suffocate if you lie him on his back."

By the time she started bringing my fat aunt Alma with her, I'd had it. They perked a pot of coffee, broke open an Entenmann's coffee cake and gave detailed infant histories of every one of their children. "Jerry was colicky, kept me up six months straight, but Willie, God bless'm, slept eight hours the first night."

"That's like Beverly. You were the best baby. Never a peep. Loved to sleep. You're lucky Jason's like that. You don't know. Your brother—up every night. I didn't mind, though. You get attached. Wait. You'll see."

One day, around the same time I first smelled winter in the air, I sat at the table with my mother and aunt and Jason, who was in his little seat on top of the table. I watched my aunt's fat fingers roll a cake crumb on her plate and couldn't take them another minute. I stood up and said, "I'm bringing Jason to the library."

"You can't," my mother said. "You can't take a baby in public until he's had all his shots."

"You said I could after six weeks. I'm going crazy."

"Then you go. I'll watch him."

"No."

"You can't take him, and that's the end of it."

"He's *my baby*."

"It's awfully breezy," my aunt said. "Might be hard to catch his breath." She shrugged and bit her lips.

I ignored her, put a jacket and bonnet on Jason,

then made a triangle out of a blanket and wrapped him up.

At the library, I checked out *David Copperfield,* and when I returned, my mother had lost her stand as big chief the baby expert. I invited my girlfriends over every night. Virginia was commuting to college. The rest had jobs, except for Fay, who was pregnant and still living down in New London. I felt sorry for Fay, but I figured it was my duty not to deceive her and to tell her the truth about the horrors of childbirth when she visited. "It hurts like hell," I said to Fay and Beatrice and Virginia as we drank coffee one night in the kitchen. "That miracle shit is a bunch of propaganda. I'll never, no matter what, have another one as long as I live. And Jason? He's all right. I love him, but it's not what you imagine. It's more like you'd love an abandoned puppy you found on the street."

With my friends around, I liked to make fun of Jason. I took off his clothes, strapped him to his changing table, then imitated Diana Ross in my "Love Child" routine. "Started his life in old cold run-down tenement slum . . . love child, always second best, love child, different from the rest." I swung my hips, spun around, and pointed at him to the beat.

If we laughed too loud, Raymond called from the living room for us to keep it down.

By winter, Ray was working four to twelve and leaving me alone every night. And just about every night, Virginia came by to keep me company after she'd finished her homework. She gave me all her books to read as soon as she'd finished them, like *The Ego and the Id,* from Psychology 101, and some Hemingway, Fitzgerald, and Ford Madox Ford books from a course called "The Jazz Age." I joined the Literary

Guild and got four more books by Hemingway, four by Steinbeck, and four by Faulkner, which I read whenever Jase went down for a nap or I could get him to shut up in his playpen for a while. I was trying to make myself smart to make up for not going to college.

The thing V and I liked to do best, besides talk about her classes, was to play with the Ouija board. Usually, we asked it questions like if I'd ever get divorced; when Raymond would die; if Jason would go to college; when Bobby and Virginia would marry; how many children they'd have; and if Bobby would make it home from Vietnam in one piece. Then one night we contacted a spirit. Her name was Nancy and she told us her history: she'd died at the age of eighteen, had three brothers still alive and one sister dead, lived somewhere in Michigan, and was a B student in high school. We carried on a dialogue with Nancy for a couple of nights before she turned nasty.

It was early spring and one of those moonless nights when little puffs of wind pushed the shades away from the window, leaving a black gap where someone could peek in. We were a little scared to begin with, but then when the magic indicator started jerking around the board spelling out profanities, I thought my heart would beat a hole through my chest. "Nancy, is that you?" I said.

Fuck, bitch, bastard, asshole.

"Why are you swearing?" Virginia asked.

Dirty twat, scum, cunt.

Then we heard a crash behind us. We jerked our hands off the magic indicator. The utensil rack was swinging from one screw in the wall and the utensils were strewn all over the floor.

We walked over to the wall to get a good look.

Here's the thing. The rack was made in such a way that you had to squeeze it together to pull the round holes over the screws. The only way it could be swinging there would be if the other screw had fallen out of the wall or if someone had squeezed the rack together, then pulled it off. Both screws were still in the wall.

V and I looked at each other, screamed, ran up the stairs, and locked ourselves in the bathroom. We sat on the floor with our backs pressed against the door. "What about Jason?" V said.

"Oh God," I said. "We have to get him." We ran across the hall on our toes, went into his room, locked the door, and peeked in his crib. He was lying on his back. His eyes were wide open with only the whites showing.

We ran back into the bathroom. "He's possessed," I said.

"Oh, Mary, Mother of God." V was my only religious friend. She went to mass every morning—she said it was for the peace and quiet, but I knew she probably prayed for Bobby. Just then we heard banging at the front door. We stopped breathing. Then we heard banging at the back door, next the cellar hatchway being pulled open, then footfalls on the stairs. By the time the door opened from the cellar to the living room, we were weeping. "Bev," I heard. It was Raymond. He'd lost his keys.

We ran down the stairs and told him everything. He looked at the baby and said his eyes were normal. Then I looked, too, and they were.

Virginia was too spooked to drive home, so she slept on the sofa. The next night, she was back in our kitchen. "Nancy went nuts because of Bobby," she said. "He's dead."

"What?"

"Shrapnel. They said he didn't feel a thing. His mother called. It'll take a couple of days for his body to come home."

"You're kidding," I said.

"Right. I made it up. It's a big joke."

"I'm sorry. I didn't mean . . ." I said.

Virginia started crying. I couldn't think of a single thing to say. I wished I could cry too. I hugged her and we rocked, stretched between our seats. When Ray came home, he sat in the rocker to take off his work boots, and we told him the news. He threw a boot across the floor, then flung himself back, pressed the heels of his hands into his eyes, and said, "My buddy. My buddy."

The night before the funeral, Ray and I didn't put Jase to bed at six o'clock as usual. We sat on our steps, and Jason, eight months old now, pushed a dump truck around our feet. We put the "White Album" on and, one by one, as if they'd been invited, people began to pull into our driveway and park on the road. There were about a dozen of us sitting on our steps and lying on our lawn that night, listening to the Beatles, reminiscing about Bobby. He'd gone to Dag Hammarskjold with me and had been responsible for the rash of bomb scares one freezing fall. The whole school had to stand outside while the cops searched every locker and desk in the building. A guy named Lenny flicked a cigarette into the night and told us how he'd been waiting for his turn outside the vice-principal's office when Bobby called the vice-principal an ape, then decked him. Bobby was expelled for that one. Rather than face his father, he ran away to Maine and got a severe case of frostbite. But then in high school, he'd joined the football team, and made more touchdowns than anyone. His father was proud of him. Which was Virginia's theory of why he joined the marines: to keep his father that way.

On leave after boot camp, Bobby'd come over for Sunday dinner. He hardly ate any macaroni, then he drank so much he puked in the living room. After he'd come downstairs from washing his face, I'd asked him if he was scared to go to war.

"Bev," Ray said.

"What?"

"You don't ask a guy those questions."

"Oh," I'd said, and Bobby turned his face away.

Sitting on the steps, I pictured Bobby the way he'd looked at my wedding, wearing a shirt with huge polka dots and maroon bell-bottoms. Then I pictured him in the photo he'd sent me from Nam. He had a rifle slung over his shoulder and his hair cut like a Mohican. He was standing on a hill and looked like a statue. I wondered if I'd still remember Bobby when I was thirty or forty. I'd be an adult, but in my memory he'd still be a kid. I wondered if Bobby would've always been wild or if he'd have calmed down, settled in a job somewhere, had a couple of kids, a bald head, a beer belly. I wondered if Bobby was the lucky one. I looked at the back of my son's neck—he was passed out on the grass. It looked so delicate, so tender. Finally, I wept.

"Blackbird" was playing in the background, and I thought how Bobby would never get the chance to spread his wings and learn to fly. I wondered if any of us would.

CHAPTER 6

A year after that—in June 1970, to be exact—at the tail end of the most glorious spring of my youth, if you can still consider the age of nineteen youth, my heart broke.

The thing that got me, the real kick in the ass, was I was happy. Really happy. Marriage was working, because marijuana had changed our lives. Not only did Ray and I dress differently—we both wore sunglasses (we called them shades) day and night, and bell-bottom jeans that were so long they dragged on the ground and frayed on the bottoms—but we had a dream: to live *Easy Rider*. Raymond had even borrowed a thousand dollars from the credit union to buy a chopped Harley-Davidson, then managed to get laid off so we could hang out together and collect unemployment. He'd also become tight with a bunch of guys from the Animal Pack, the local motorcycle gang. I could take or leave the Animals—obviously, they were nothing like Peter Fonda and Dennis Hopper—but the important thing was I was dreaming again. There was California, there were communes, there was free love for married people. Not to mention how beautiful the world looked, in the spring, under the influence of drugs. I began to write poems.

My mother thought I'd gone off the deep end. I'd

regained my independence. I was different from her. So what if I was disorganized and a slob, I was imaginative and a thinker. "Jason," she said when he stuck his finger in his nose at a year and a half. "Get your finger out of your nose."

"Leave him alone, Ma."

"What, you're not going to teach him manners?"

"If everybody picked their nose when they felt like it, everybody would be a lot happier. You pick your nose, I pick my nose, everybody picks their nose, so why hide it? We got ruined from socialization."

"You're saying I should've let you pick your nose?"

"Yes."

"Honest to God, Beverly, I don't know who you take after."

And my father, never a slouch when it came to detective work, took one look at the cars that ended up in our driveway at all hours and knew exactly what was going on in our house. He refused to set foot in it. Which was fine with us, since he was a cop and we were doing illegal drugs.

Raymond finally had friends, so instead of sitting alone in the living room and not playing Scrabble with my friends in the kitchen because he felt too stupid, he had guys to go out with. Plus, he had long hair and a beard and was handsome. Sometimes when there was company, I'd sit across from him in a miniskirt and I'd catch the way he looked at me and want to leap across the room and land on top of him.

It was almost as though Ray and I were single. Life was blissful. One night I'd go out with my friends, and Raymond would baby-sit. The next night Ray'd go out with his, and I'd baby-sit. My friends and I rode around town smoking superb red marijuana sent from Vietnam. The air through our windows smelled of damp earth. We were awed by each leaf flapping separately on the trees. We peed in cornfields and ran through sprinklers on golf courses.

I even had a crush that spring. His name was Peter Dodd. Raymond had met him at the Crystal Spa and told me about this guy who'd shot off his toe in Vietnam to get discharged, which made him a hero to us because we thought the war was bullshit. Peter wasn't only missing a toe, he'd been born with only one testicle. I fell in love before I even laid eyes on him, then fixed him up with Beatrice. He was tall and skinny and drove a school bus. He wrote songs. Some mornings he'd pull his yellow bus across my front lawn and we'd sit in the kitchen eating toast and drinking coffee, Jason on Peter's lap. We talked about people. I read him my poems, which were very short: "Lemon days alone and lost. What will happen in the dark?" That was one. "Swing high. Swing low. Never know. Where to go." That was another. Sometimes at night with Raymond, Peter sang us his songs and I read them my poems. I felt a little sorry for Raymond because all he did most of the time was listen, but he didn't seem to mind. He nodded out in the rocker, and I watched Peter fold his long legs this way and that as we passed a joint back and forth and Peter laughed at things I said. We talked until dawn many nights. I looked at Raymond, asleep by then in the rocker, and I felt tender.

That sleeping in the rocker was the beginning of the problem. Or the beginning of my noticing there was a problem at all. Raymond had taken to half sleeping in the rocker for hours and hours, kind of scratching his nose, which was peeling from all the rubbing, and sitting there with his head on his chest nodding out. Since it often happened when we were smoking marijuana, I thought maybe it was giving Raymond brain damage. But since I was so happy, I didn't pay much attention until one night.

Beatrice and I had gone to the Coleman Brothers' carnival and I'd left Ray at home baby-sitting and expecting some friends to come over. Ever since I was a little kid, I'd loved the carnival. I had this friend, when I was very little, named Joannie Devon, who lived on top of some rickety ill-lighted stairs in a shabby apartment alone with her mother. Rumor had it that her mother had had an affair with a carnie who left town and her pregnant with Joannie. Joannie was very poor but extremely beautiful. And even as a little child, though I couldn't put a word to it, I knew Joannie had grace. There was something in the way she looked at you and moved and smiled that I thought saintly. In other words, if the Virgin Mary were going to appear to anybody, it would be Joannie. We moved away from our first house and I lost track of her. But I remembered her every time the Coleman Brothers came to town. Then I'd look at all those carnies in their booths with tattoos on their arms and voices daring you on and I'd wonder which one had fathered Joannie Devon, the angel.

Beatrice and I smoked some pot, then rode the Ferris wheel. Then we saw a trailer advertising Siamese twins. Inside there were two boys around my age, attached at the hips. They sat back to back watching the same shows on separate TVs. The pink printed sheet we were handed at the door said they were born that way and that their parents had put them in the carnival to help pay for college. The twins just sat there, their eyes riveted on their TVs, as though they were completely unaware that hundreds of people were walking behind a rope in their living room, gawking. I felt so sad after I saw those twins, I wanted to cry. The twins,

I knew, would never go to college. I got the idea that maybe the next day I could drop by, real early, before the carnival opened, and make friends with them. Have a real talk, maybe about books. I didn't tell Beatrice any of this. I just said I felt depressed. She said, "Me too."

We drove back to my house, where Peter Dodd had said he might stop later.

Ocho Perez's truck was in the driveway, which meant some of the guys from the Animal Pack were probably with Raymond.

When we walked in, Raymond was in the rocker and three guys dressed in black and blue sat shoulder to shoulder on the couch. I only knew Ocho Perez, who was in the middle, his thumbs in his belt, his head on his chest, snoozing with everyone else. Raymond heard the screen door slam, pulled his head up, opened his eyes, which took a while to focus, then he blinked at the TV. It was flashing silver specks. "Hey, man," he said. "Why don't one a you change the fucking channel?"

"Why don't you change the channel, man?" Ocho said when he pulled his head up too.

"It's my house, man. My TV. You want to watch it, you change it."

"For Christ's sake," I said, embarrassed at Raymond's rudeness. "What channel do you want? I'll change it."

"Shit, Bev," Ray said. "You home?"

I whispered to Beatrice in the kitchen that I thought the pot was making Raymond retarded.

"Do you think it can?" Beatrice asked.

"I don't know. Maybe. But they're all like that. Look at them."

"Maybe they're just tired," she said.

"I don't know what from. None of them work."

"What's dat show?" one of the guys said.

"I don't know," Raymond said.

"Ain't that Clint Eastwood?"

"Shit, man," Ocho said. "If that's Clint Eastwood, I'm John Wayne."

"John Wayne?" Raymond guffawed. "Try Sal Mineo." Ocho was small and dark and Puerto Rican, just about the only one in town.

"That ain't Clint Eastwood, man. That's what's his face," the other guy said. "You know, man. *The Rifleman.*"

"That was a good show," Raymond said.

"It sucked," Ocho said.

I rolled my eyes at Beatrice.

Peter Dodd came in the front door, and Raymond said, "Pete, my man." The guys on the couch just looked at him.

"Hey, Ray, how's it going," Pete said. "Bev, Beatrice." He smiled, walking toward the kitchen. The guys on the sofa obviously didn't know or didn't like Peter, and vice versa. This made me uneasy.

I decided it was time Raymond found some work and stopped hanging out with the Animal Pack.

The next day I suggested he look for some kind of part-time job, maybe under the table so he could still collect unemployment, and mentioned that the motorcycle we'd been hotly awaiting seemed stalled indefinitely. Ray's reports on the state of the bike went like this: First the guy wasn't sure he wanted to sell it after all; then Raymond decided the guy should fix the exhaust before we handed over any money; then the guy cracked up the front fender and didn't have the bucks to fix it; and on and on. I told Ray we should take this opportunity to stockpile some money for our trip across country.

To my surprise, Raymond agreed with me and went out nearly every day looking for work. It was a drag not to have a car and boring to be stuck home alone with Jason again. There was only so much you could do with such a little kid. We danced to *Sgt. Pepper,* the "White Album," *Abbey Road.* I lay on the floor and he sat on my belly. I pushed his features around like his skin was made of Play-Doh. He touched his finger to my eye and said, "Nose." I said, "Eye." We played patty cake, this little piggy, itsy bitsy spider. He tried to sing along. I bent my knees and stood him on my feet and lifted him high in the air like an acrobat, which made him laugh and fall forward so I'd catch him. Jason spent as many waking hours on my lap as off it. When he napped, I read and then reread *Rebecca* and dreamed about living in a mansion and having no children, just a maid who ran my bath while I sat at my desk every morning and answered letters with a gold pen.

Then one day Ray left home around noon as usual and didn't return till nine in the evening. I was a little worried, but mostly I was bored to death and had such a craving for a Dairy Queen ice cream cone I thought I'd go out of my mind. Of course there was no way to get a Dairy Queen without a car or a baby-sitter, and watching that clock creep forward little by little, later and later, while I envisioned that vanilla cone with chocolate sprinkles, made me furious. I was beside myself. It wasn't like this was the only time he'd been too late for dinner lately, and always with some lame excuse like a flat tire. I was so pissed I couldn't sit still. I thumbed through an old *Life* magazine that had pictures of all the dead soldiers who got it that week, but I couldn't concentrate. I sat on the front stoop, but the Uglies were planting things on their side of the yard, so I went back in and shuffled through our records. I pulled out the Jefferson Airplane album Raymond had bought. We'd had an agreement that we couldn't buy anything because money was too tight. I said, "Raymond, I thought we agreed."

"I didn't buy it. Ocho gave it to me."

"He just gave you a brand new record?" It was still sealed in cellophane.

"It was a present," he said. Later I found a receipt from Spinner Records in his pocket. There were other records too—Jimi Hendrix, The Who, Led Zeppelin, but they were used. Did Ocho Perez really just lay them on Raymond out of the goodness of his Animal Pack heart?

Thinking like this just added fuel to the fire, so when Ray finally rolled in, I was fuming. I ran to the door and locked it.

Ray broke the window with his fist to unlock it.

I thought about the Uglies watching outside and would've giggled if I wasn't so crazy with fury. I stomped into the kitchen, then handed Raymond a whisk broom and dustpan. He took it and began sweeping glass when he realized what he was doing and dropped the broom like a hot potato. "I don't believe it. You fucking lock me out of my own house. My fucking hand's bleeding. Then you give me a broom to sweep it up? You are a bitch, you know that?"

"Where were you, Raymond?" I said, determined not to believe a word he said.

"What is this, the Inquisition?"

"Let me guess. You ran over a dog and had to bring it to a vet."

"I don't have to take this." He turned around and left.

Why did he always get the car? Wasn't it both of

ours? I kicked myself for not taking off first. I could've gotten a Dairy Queen, then gone to visit Beatrice.

From the moment Ray left until the moment he walked through the door at midnight, hunger, boredom, and frustration worked together to clear my head. I knew like a clairvoyant that Ray hadn't been looking for work the past weeks and had probably been getting screwed up every day. I decided when Raymond returned I would talk to him calmly and maybe he'd tell me the truth.

When Raymond returned he bumped into the hassock, then slumped into the rocker. "You'll never guess who I talked to tonight," he said.

"Look, Raymond," I said. "I don't care if you don't get a job. I've been thinking I like it better when you're home anyway. But you've been lying, haven't you?"

"Your old boyfriend Robby Costa . . ." I stopped short. Robby Costa was the first boy I'd ever kissed. I was in the eighth grade and we kissed on a hammock, then the next day when we went for a walk, he held my hand and rubbed his middle finger up and down my palm. It made me nauseous and I never went out with him again. "Robby Costa was not my boyfriend," I said.

"That's not what he says. He says, 'That old lady of yours is a nice piece of ass.'"

I just looked at him.

"How am I supposed to feel when some guy tells me my old lady's a nice piece of ass? That's why I got fucked up."

"You're making this up."

"Were you really a virgin or were you lying?"

I threw the first thing that came to hand, which happened to be Jason's workbench with different-colored pegs. I threw it as hard as I could at his head. He deflected it with a forearm.

"Are you saying I wasn't a virgin?" I was screaming now.

"All I want to know's how am I supposed to feel?"

"How *you* feel?" I threw the contents of Jason's toy box one by one. Raymond tried his best to dodge them. "I was a goddamn virgin when I fucked you and got fucking pregnant and ruined my life. You lousy son of a bitch. How dare you come in here and tell me some ass-wipe moron imbecile told you I'm a pig. Why didn't you punch him out? You're a wimp and a retard. I should've killed myself before I ever married you." I was crying uncontrollably now. I was pummeling him with my fists now. He was backed up against the wall, blocking my blows. "Jesus, Beverly," he said. "I'm sorry. I'm sorry. I didn't know you'd get so upset." I believed I could beat him up, tear him limb from limb, kill him with my bare hands, but he really looked sorry, and scared. I ran out the door and peeled out. I had to stop every mile or so because I was crying so hard I couldn't see. I decided to kill myself and drove around looking for the right spot.

I found it by the old reservoir. A huge oak. But then I thought, What if I ram the car into it and I just total it then we won't have any wheels, and I might get arrested and my father would kill me. Then I thought, And what about Jason? Do I want him to be raised by Raymond? To use double negatives when he speaks? Raymond probably wouldn't even raise him. He'd give him to my parents or, worse, his mother. I got out of the car, leaned against the tree, then slid down the oak and sat with my back against it. Raymond obviously had brought up Robby Costa to deflect any blame from himself for not looking for work and for lying, and I'd fallen for it. But that Raymond could stoop so low as to accuse me of not being a virgin, when it was sex with him that had ruined my life, was unforgivable.

It was dawn when I got into bed.

"Hon?" he said.

I didn't answer.

"I'm sorry."

I ignored him.

"I know you were a virgin."

Silence.

"I don't know why I said that. I'm a loser. I'm no good. I wouldn't blame you if you divorced me."

"You are a loser."

"You hate me."

Silence.

"Bev?"

"All right. All right. All right. I don't hate you, now can I go to sleep? And you get up with Jason." Raymond fell right back to sleep. I inspected his arm for needle tracks, but there weren't any.

When I got up at noon, Raymond looked like a ghost and so did Jason. Jason's forehead was hot, so I took his temperature. It was one hundred degrees. I gave Raymond our last money—which was five dollars, until he got his unemployment check in a couple of days—to pick up some baby aspirin and orange juice. This was noon. By four o'clock he still hadn't shown, which I was figuring was grounds for murder, but Raymond wasn't that much of a creep. Something bad must've happened. I was worried. Finally, the phone rang. It was my mother. "Bev, your father called from the station. He has Raymond with him," she said.

I pictured him handcuffed in a cell.

She said my father was coming home with Raymond and that he wanted to talk to me. She would pick me up.

I put on Jason's sweater. His cheeks were flushed. Jason might grow up and say, My father is an ex-con. In a way, it was Jason's fault. He should've never been born. I hugged him to me and felt his hot face against my neck and his hands holding on to my shoulders while I waited for my mother. When I walked out of the house, she moved to the passenger's side so I could drive and she could hold Jason. "Poor honey," she said, taking off his hat and pushing his hair away from his face. "You coming to your Mimi's? I made you some chicken soup. We can put pastina in just like you like it. Poor baby. It's awful when your throat hurts."

"Ma, what do you think this is about?"

"I don't know a thing."

Why was she so worried about Jason and not worried about me?

I left Jase with my mother and went down into the basement recreation room, where Ray and my father were sitting in chairs, not talking. I sat on the couch and my father nodded to Raymond. "He has something he wants to tell you," he said.

Raymond stared at my knees as he said, "I spent the money for Jase's aspirin on dope. My son's sick, and I spent the money on dope."

"What dope?"

"Heroin."

"You're a junkie?"

He nodded his head. "I went to your father for help. I'm no good, Beverly."

"You went to the police station?"

"He wanted to talk to me. He's sick, Bev," my father said.

"Where are the tracks?" He turned his arm palm upward and exhibited a purple scar on the cleft of his left arm. I'd looked at his right.

"We're going to help him straighten out," my father said.

I could only breathe in short spurts. All I could think was, This is a coward's maneuver. He was scared to face me alone, so he'd gone to my father for protection. How could I be mad at him with the representative of the law, and my own father, on his side? And why was my father sticking up for him, anyway? What about the time he called me to the station and believed some stupid jerk instead of me? Tried to bully me into admitting I was drinking? Threatened me with a lie detector? What was this anyway? Guys against girls?

"How?" I asked.

"They got a program at the hospital in Meriden. Maybe we could get him in. He's got to stop smoking that marijuana, too. No drinking. He needs to get a job. Keep busy."

What about me, Dad? What will you do to help me? I wanted to say, but never would. I'd never in my life had the courage to say what was in my heart to my father.

On the ride home, Ray opened the glove compartment, pulled out his harmonica case, and said, "Open it." It contained a hypodermic needle. "That's where I keep my works. You know the belt hanging on the hook in the bathroom? That's what I used to tie off." I pictured the times his friends went off to the bathroom, one by one, and took too long for pissing. I pictured myself driving around on winding roads with my girlfriends while Raymond tucked Jason in, then stuck a needle in his vein.

"The thousand dollars for the Harley?" he said. "Spent it all." Then he started crying.

"You spent the thousand dollars!" There went the dream.

"I bought some of that Panama red. I was partners with Cal and the son of a bitch ripped me off. He claims somebody stole it. I'm a loser, Bev."

No shit.

He told me that at first a nickel was enough. But then he needed more. He broke into houses. He stole money and TV sets, a couple of stereos. I pictured me and my friends eating jelly muffins in the kitchen and Raymond with a stocking over his face climbing in a window. "Did you steal albums?"

He nodded.

"All them days I was looking for jobs? Dope," he said.

I pictured Raymond going to the beach with the Animal Pack, sitting shoulder to shoulder in the water nodding out.

"I'm sorry, Bev," he said. "I fucked up." Then he started crying again.

"I will try to help you, Raymond," I said, feeling betrayed to the bone, thinking, I will never believe another word out of your mouth. "I will really try. But one more time, one more lie, and it's over." I was half wishing he'd screw up that one more time.

"I won't lie, Bev. I promise."

"Promise on Jason's life."

"That's stupid."

"No it's not. Promise on Jason's life that you will never lie again."

"Okay, I promise."

"Say it."

"I promise on Jason's life I won't lie."

Raymond hadn't been a junkie long enough to need a padded cell like in the movies. But the next day he had the chills and a runny nose. I made Lipton soup· and dropped an egg in it. Ray shivered under a blanket and took tiny sips from a cup. When Beatrice called to come over, I told her we were sick. Ray put his feet in my lap and I rubbed them.

I figured the first couple of weeks would be the hardest, so I stayed with him twenty-four hours a day. I played martyr, which isn't hard when you've been raised by an Italian mother. I stopped smoking pot and drinking, too. I even let Raymond watch his TV shows without arguing. We sat Jase in the car seat between us and rode around town picking out our favorite houses, pointing out moo cows and horses to Jason. Then Ray found a job landscaping for two brothers. I dropped him off every morning, then at noon I drove back to where he was clipping hedges or mowing a lawn or digging a hole in the sun. We sat under a tree on the grass and ate the sandwiches I'd made. We didn't say much, just watched the cars go past and Jason pick dandelions.

After a couple of weeks, Ray said, "Bev, no offense, but the guys are calling me pussy-whipped. Maybe you shouldn't bring me lunch anymore." Two weeks later, Ray didn't bring money home on pay day. He said the brothers hadn't been paid so they couldn't pay him.

The next week it was the same story.

The following week, I was lying on the grass while Jase filled up cups and emptied them in his plastic pool when the phone rang. It was Virginia. She said, "Bev, I know it's none of my business, but I don't think Ray has that job anymore."

"What do you mean?"

"His car's at the Crystal Spa. It was there yesterday too. Did he tell you he was working?"

There wasn't enough time to answer between breaths.

"I got to go, V," I said.

I collapsed onto the couch and sobbed. Then I remembered Jase in the pool and stopped crying as suddenly as I'd begun. After all, I'd be better off without Raymond. Who wanted to marry him to begin with? Really, it was a godsend. I could divorce him and be exonerated. No one would blame me. If I were still a Catholic, I could probably get an annulment.

I went outside and turned the hose on. I ran cold water over my face, then walked back to Jason. Jase splashed his hands on top of the water in his pool. "I'm going to kick your father out," I said.

Jase stood up and splashed back down, laughing.

"You won't have a father. You'll have divorced parents."

Jason picked up a red cup and threw it out of the pool, then looked at me. I squirted water at a cat, which fluffed out its tail and darted under the dead bush.

"We won't have any money," I said, and moved my face closer to Jason's. "We won't have any food." I moved my face closer and crinkled my nose like a witch's. "We'll starve to death."

"No," Jason said, turning his back and trying to climb out. He slipped back in and started crying. I started crying. I sat in the pool with my clothes on. Jason sat on my lap.

"It'll be just you and me," I said.

CHAPTER 7

"THIS is unfortunate." The young social worker with thick glasses and chubby cheeks bounced his pencil on my application and smiled. "But you won't be on welfare long. When your son's old enough, you'll get a job. I'm sure of it. Unfortunately, some people come to view welfare as a, well, a crutch." Then for some reason—he was bored, he liked me, he liked to hear himself talk—he took an hour to describe his caseload and the problems he faced: the utter impossibility of getting these people's feet off the ground. The majority, he said, were either former citizens of Agua, Puerto Rico, who settled near their families in Meriden and spoke no English, had no skills and no interest in working, or the wives of formerly unemployed men, who'd traveled south from Maine to find work in factories. Once they got their jobs, they had more money than they knew what to do with, so they spent it drinking in bars, eventually becoming hopeless alcoholics who were known to beat their wives. Then, for one reason or another, the men deserted and their wives stayed and, I guess, had to come listen to this guy too. I wondered what he talked about to them. When he finished his talk, he said, "But obviously, you're different." He smiled again and winked at me. Then I signed some papers and was told

I could expect enough money for rent, utilities, food stamps, plus what averaged out to be about five dollars' spending money each week.

I appreciated the guy's vote of confidence, but when I was a kid and pictured myself being interviewed, it was by Johnny Carson or Merv Griffin, not a social worker. I was disappointed in myself, but I wasn't complaining. One week before, I'd thought I might be forced to ask my parents if Jase and I could live with them, when number one, there wasn't enough room, and number two, my father had said, "Once you leave this house, you're not coming back," and number three, I'd rather die than be reduced to living by my parents' rules again.

Ray, however, had no qualms about moving in with his mother. After I told him to get out, he stuffed his clothes into two pillowcases, said, "It's better this way. I'm glad it's over," then let the door slam behind him on his way to his mother's. Soon the credit union repossessed his car, which was formerly our car, and Ray landed on the town green nodding out and crying to anyone who'd listen, "I lost my car. I lost my son. I lost my wife," in exactly that order.

The guy was falling apart. It hurt my eyes to look at him. Whenever he managed to keep a date and pick up Jason for an outing, he'd stand on the other side of the screen door, his pants falling from his hips and his neck like a skinned chicken's. He hid his eyes behind mirrored sunglasses. His voice was thick with drugs. He nodded his head and said one word—"Bev."

Meanwhile Jason, who was twenty months old now, would be running from the door to me as soon as he saw him, saying, "Daddy's here. Daddy's here." Then I watched from the window as Ray tilted Jason into the car and next to whatever Animal he'd recruited to drive him and Jason to the community pool or Dairy Queen or Hubbard Park to feed the ducks.

The first time we said more than two words to each other was in public, a month after we'd split up. It was at Big Top Hamburgers, a hood hangout, where my girlfriends and I used to cruise Friday nights after we got bored with the collegiates at the Farm Shop.

I practically had to fall down on my knees to get my mother to baby-sit for me. "Men see a divorced woman and they're out for one thing," she said.

"For Christ's sake, Ma. I'm going to the *movies* with *Beatrice*."

"They figure once a woman's had it," she kept going.

"Had *what*?" I wanted her to come out and say it.

"You know what I'm talking about."

"No. Tell me."

"Once a woman knows what it's like, she wants it. Men can sense it."

"Like dogs in heat?"

"Don't be disgusting."

Look who's talking about being disgusting. "Ma," I said, as calmly as I could, then waited a beat between each word. "Just say yes."

After she said she'd have to think about it, which meant ask my father, she agreed to take Jason overnight on Wednesday. A weekend night was out of the question.

Beatrice and I went to see *M.A.S.H.* at the new movie theater forty minutes away, then smoked pot as we drove and listened to all of *Tommy*, which a radio station was playing uninterrupted. The air hit my face from the open window. I got a whiff of spring, damp and potent, and thought, I'm free. Right now, Beatrice and I could go to Big Top Hamburgers and hang out all night. I have no husband, and my parents would never know it. I could have a rare charcoal-broiled burger. I could actually flirt with some guys in the parking lot. Which was exactly what we did: order a charcoal-broiled burger, rare. But I never got the chance to flirt, because Raymond, the newborn derelict, showed up, weaved into the building, and said without stopping for air, "Where's my son?"

I saw red. What nerve. Raymond probably went to Big Top Hamburgers every night of the week, and now he was insinuating I wasn't taking good care of *his* son? "In the trunk of the car. Where do you think?" I felt people turn on their stools to look at me.

"I'm serious," he demanded.

"It's none of your business," I said.

"I'm his old man."

"Father. Say father." I knew I should shut up, but I couldn't stop. "If you're such a good father, tell me what your son's new word is? You don't even know. Where the fuck were you Sunday? What makes you think you're entitled to know anything about him?"

"He better have a baby-sitter."

"Bev," Beatrice said, and opened her eyes wide as if to say, Let's get the hell out of here.

I brushed past Raymond, got into Beatrice's car, and she drove out of the parking lot so fast my grape soda tipped in my lap.

So much for hanging out at Raymond's spots.

Eventually, though, we cooled down enough to make small talk whenever he dropped by, mostly about Jason and people we both knew. Then one night late in August, almost three months after Ray and I'd split up, I heard a light knocking at my front door. I'd fallen asleep reading *A Tree Grows in Brooklyn* and got up to look out the window. I could see Raymond from above. He was standing on the front stoop looking at his feet. When I answered the door, I realized I should've put something over my nightgown, because I saw Raymond's eyes drift over my breasts from the other side of the screen.

"I have to talk to you," he said.

I opened the door, and crossed my arms on my chest as I sat on the sofa and he sat on the chair across from me, his knees wide open. He took a pack of Luckies from his shirt pocket, shook out a cigarette, and lit it. The way his wrist and fingers moved, where he put the cigarette between his lips, and the way he pulled the cigarette away so his lips kind of stuck to the filter were so familiar, I hugged my heart to protect myself from getting reinvolved.

"Bev," he repeated. "I got something I have to talk to you about."

I nodded.

"I volunteered for Nam. The 101st Airborne Division. I'll be a paratrooper."

"What! Why?"

"I don't know." He shrugged and looked away. "I don't know. Bobby died over there, and I don't know. I got nothing going for me here. I figured I should defend my country."

"But you don't believe in the war."

"I figure, my country's in it, I should fight. And besides, I don't have you no more, or Jason."

"You have Jason. He's your son."

He stared at his hands and shook his head.

I resisted the urge to pull his head to my chest and rock him.

That night I stared at the ceiling in the dark. When I first knew Raymond, he drove a yellow Bonneville with a black roof and had plenty of money for beer and pizza, the outdoor movies, or Riverside Amusement Park. He was living with his mother then, too. He was planning to maybe join the navy to get his high school equivalency and a skill like electronics. Then I got pregnant and his life was ruined. I wept imagining Raymond thousands of miles from home, scrunched down in some rice paddy to avoid the bombs raining shrapnel over his head. I wept harder when I thought of Bobby's wake. The coffin was closed because Bobby's body had been too old. His family had placed his graduation picture on a little shelf above, so we could all remember what he looked like. Raymond wouldn't have a graduation picture to put above his coffin.

In the morning I woke up as usual to Jason calling, "Mommy." I lifted him out and changed his diaper. I hugged him and smelled the Johnson No More Tears baby shampoo in his hair as I carried him down the stairs. I put him down in the kitchen and he walked straight to the cupboard, put his hand on the knob, and looked at me to check if I would say no or not. Then he began emptying the pans out for the first time of the day. I made us some cinnamon toast, then cut his into strips and put him in his high chair. He said, "Mmmm good," as he daintily picked up the first strip and took a bite. "Good?" he said, prompting me to say my line.

"Mmmm, good," I said, biting my toast and realizing I had no appetite. I had a picture in my mind of Raymond standing in the hospital room looking afraid, holding the ceramic rabbit. The ivy plant had died almost immediately. I had no idea what I'd done with the bunny vase. Then I had another picture of Jason the week before, standing on the rocker in front of the window looking down the street for his father, who never showed. Jason's father was a liar and a junkie.

I handed Jason his plastic cup of juice. He took a sip, his eyes watering, and handed the cup back. It became crystal clear. Raymond was going to Vietnam for the heroin, the abundant, pure, and cheap heroin. He wasn't going to Vietnam to defend his country and avenge Bobby's death. He was going there because it was easier than staying here. Besides, who knew with Raymond. It could've all been a ploy to get me feeling sorry for him, to get me to open my arms and say, Don't go. Come back. I called Raymond up.

"Raymond," I said. "I've been thinking. If you go to Vietnam, Jason'll be almost three when you return. He won't remember you."

"That's true."

"What if I said to you I decided to go live in California for a year and a half, and just assumed you'd take care of Jason?"

"That's different."

"No it's not. You can't just leave him for me to take care of."

"I'm going to defend my country."

"Bullshit. You're going so you can afford to be a junkie."

There was silence on the line.

Jason crammed the last strip of toast in his mouth and said, "More." I gave him mine. "Raymond, you have a son. I've been thinking. Either you stay and make up your mind that you're taking responsibility for Jason, or you give him up. Don't come back after Vietnam."

"He'd probably be better off."

I didn't disagree.

"You know me. I'm a fuck-up. I'm as bad as my old man."

"So you're giving him up."

"He'll be better off."

"I got to go."

I wiped Jason's face and his sticky fingers with a washcloth, then released him from the high chair. He went to the cardboard box filled with toys in the living room. I watched him as he dug through the box and came up with a golf ball, which he rolled to me.

I'd read up on kids of divorced parents and how they tended to think they drove the deserting parent away. I would be sure to tell Jason it wasn't his fault. I'd tell him his father and I had fights and didn't get along. I would not make Raymond into a bad person. I'd tell Jason his father wanted to go fight for his country. I'd tell him his father was brave. I could even tell him his father died and that's why he never came back. But that would definitely be a mistake. Jason may have inherited his father's lying genes, and I'd better set a good example. Raymond's mother had told me that Raymond's father was the same as Raymond, lying for the pleasure of it. I'd rather have Jason turn into a drooling idiot. I'd tell Jason the truth about all things. I'd tell Jason his father was a drug addict who couldn't help himself. I'd tell Jason the way things really are, so life wouldn't slap him in the face when he grew up. At that moment, I wasn't sure if I'd even let him believe in Santa Claus.

Jason was quiet by the toy box for a minute, then I got a whiff and knew it was time to change his diaper. That made me picture a scene. It was from when Jason was an infant. Every evening when Raymond came home, the three of us would eat dinner, then Raymond would take off Jason's clothes and dip him in the kitchen sink for a bath. Sometimes I'd sit at the table, smoke a cigarette, and watch. I was mesmerized by the gentleness of Raymond's hands as they cupped water and released it over Jason's shining wet body. Some-times I'd wonder what it must be like for Jason to feel the largeness of his father's hands and the sureness as they supported his back.

My mother walked in then. I hadn't even heard her car pull up. "P.U.," she said. "Somebody stinks."

Jason laughed and made a game of running away.

"Oh no you don't," she said, dropping her pocket-book onto the couch and grabbing him. She rinsed out the washcloth, with Jason on her hip, soaped it up, then laid Jason down on the floor for a diaper change.

"So, what were you doing?" my mother said.

"Nothing," I said. "Just thinking."

"Better not think too much," she said. "Your hair'll turn gray."

CHAPTER 8

RAYMOND wrote me letters that I threw away without reading, until the one that made an even dozen. In it he'd enclosed a snapshot of himself passed out on a bed, with a hundred beer cans and empty liquor bottles jumbled on the shelves above him. His shirt was bunched up at his armpits, and his arm, displaying a tattoo of a devil holding a pitchfork, was draped across his bare belly. I guess this was his idea of sexy. He wrote, "I just saw *Love Story*. I am Oliver and you are my Jenny. I've lost you." Did he think we had this great love fit for books and movies, a tragedy to make millions weep, when I, the heroine, hadn't shed a tear since the night I pictured him floundering in a rice paddy? I ended his illusion by writing to him a few hateful words: "I don't now, never did, and never could love you, so do me a favor and forget I ever existed." Then I marched to the middle of the driveway and in a gouge in the asphalt made a pyre of his picture and letter.

The only thing I thought about marriage after that was, Never in a million years, not for a billion dollars, and never again if it kills me.

Then it was a year since Raymond deserted us, the close of the summer of 1971. Jason was about to be three, and a few days later I'd be twenty-one, drinking age, voting age, and a legal adult. I was at a picnic in Beatrice's backyard with Jason and Fay, her two-and-a-half-year-old daughter, Amelia, and a bunch of Beatrice's friends from work. Fay and I'd had a plan. We'd split a hit of acid, then once we got to Beatrice's all-girls picnic, all the girls would take care of our two kids. Problem was, we didn't let Beatrice and her friends in on the plan and they were too dense to pick up on it. First of all, they had no idea we were tripping, because they'd never tripped themselves and wouldn't know a tripping person from a lunatic, which is probably what they thought we were. And second of all, they just didn't understand. This was our logic: Fay and I had gotten knocked up, which made us the scapegoats or fall guys. In other words, if it hadn't been us it would've been them, so the least they could do was take up some slack by easing our kids off our backs during one measly picnic. No such luck.

So I'm lying on my back in Beatrice's parents' aluminum pool and I'm tripping peacefully, listening to the trees talk to me in a language I'm sure I'd understand if only I could concentrate harder. But then here comes somebody handing me my son. By the blinding orange of her bikini, I know it's Beatrice. She says, "Somebody wants to swim with his mommy."

Couldn't she tell somebody didn't want to swim with her son? But she's dangling him over the water, so I reach out to get him and he slips through my fingers and underwater. I catch him just after his face goes under, but he starts crying hysterically anyway, spitting and coughing and making me feel awful. Now I understand every word from the trees. They're saying: You're a terrible mother. You almost drowned your son. He'll remember this moment forever.

I hugged Jason and bounced him around the pool to distract him. When we climbed out, I lay on my back and Jason sat on my stomach. His head was ringed by the sun, and for a minute I thought it was a halo, but then a cloud obscured the vision and I concentrated on his face. He had three freckles on his nose and blue-gray eyes that were shaped like almonds. Did Raymond have eyes shaped like almonds too? I closed my eyes to change the subject, and what I saw was the Blessed Virgin standing on a world with the infant Jesus perched in the crook of her arm, like on a plastic card, and that's when I remembered about my mother. She said she almost drowned when she was little, even went down for the third time, but then she saw the Virgin Mary holding out her arms, and the next thing she knew she was lying in the sand, saved.

Jason had had a vision too, of an old lady floating outside his window, trying to get in. He was afraid of her. I told him she was probably a fairy.

"She's too old," he said.

"Not for a guardian angel. It's probably my great-grandmother Irene dropping by to give you good luck."

"You think so?"

"Sure."

My great-grandmother Irene was on my mind a lot these days, because every time I turned around, my mother was saying, "I don't know who you take after. Not *my* family. It must be your father's grandmother Irene." Personally, I took this as a compliment, but although my mother liked Irene, she meant it as an insult, because Irene had committed the cardinal sin of Neglecting Her Children. Irene, too, escaped from her house every chance she got. She liked to walk around the neighborhood stopping here for a cup of coffee or there to check out some other Italian immigrant who'd just landed on her block. Her favorite thing in the world was the movies, and she went every chance she got. This made her husband—who traveled around the country shooting off fireworks—furious, especially since she left her house a mess and her kids running wild. So, the story goes, one day he loaded the dirty dishes into his wheelbarrow, then pushed it straight down the center aisle of Wilkinson's Theater, to shame her. My story goes that when she saw him, she burst out laughing.

Irene's story does not have a happy ending, though. By the time I met her, her husband was dead and she'd squandered all her money, had no house, no teeth, and was a pauper. She lived with various nieces and nephews but refused to live with her own kids—maybe because she didn't like them, maybe because they tried to boss her around and trap her behind four walls. Meanwhile, my father had just become a cop, driving in his cruiser, and never did a week go by without his seeing his grandmother, dressed in black, her white hair darting from her head like dandelion spores, looking like a witch wandering on the edge of town near some cornfield or cow pasture. He'd stop to ask her if she wanted a ride, but she always refused it. Now, this was his grandmother, so he couldn't order, "Get in," like he could with me. So what he did instead—the day after he spied her at Woolworth's trying on glasses and squinting at a popcorn sign—was order a powwow with his mother and his aunts and uncles, who decided the only thing was a nursing home. When they checked her in, she refused to give up her shoes. When she died three months later, they found them hidden beneath her pillow.

I sometimes wondered, given the authority, if my

father would stick me in an institution too. Especially since he'd reverted to his old trick of stalking me. Like I said, this was 1971. I was a hippie. I wore no bra, walked barefoot, had sex indiscriminately, plus I hitch-hiked and went shoplifting with Jason. My son was the prefect lure for rides (who could refuse a white-haired three-year-old standing in a gutter next to his mother and sticking out his thumb?) and the best decoy for shoplifting (all I had to do was let him run wild in a store and the ladies were so riveted on his grubby little hands they never even noticed me, except to shoot dirty looks that meant, Will you please control your child, you stupid hippie). Probably, there were times my father and his buddies saw me sitting on the lawn of Robert Early Junior High staring at a fluorescent light thinking it was a television. Certainly, they kept track of the multitude of cars that spent the night in my driveway, not to mention the various men who drove them. I wonder if they could distinguish which guy was for Fay and which for me.

Fay and I had no problem keeping track, because we had a list stuck behind a picture of an onion skin Fay had painted and hung on the wall. Fay and Amelia had moved in with me and Jase in the springtime, after Fay had found a pair of bikini underpants in the back-seat of her car and surmised, correctly, that her husband was an adulterer. So she drove up from Pennsylvania in her yellow Dodge, dragging half her furniture behind her, and moved in. We'd thrown my old Flintstone furniture out and moved her beautiful furniture in before she'd painted the picture of the onion skin. We didn't know yet that we'd have a list to hang behind it. That started about a month after she'd moved in.

We'd been driving around town with our kids,

really happy. True, we both had failed marriages. True, we were both on welfare. True, we had little kids keeping us from hitchhiking to California or through Europe, joining a commune, and about a million other things we could be doing in the world, but here we were, best girlfriends living together with our kids. It was like a dream come true. One of my fantasies as a kid was that my best friend Donna and I and our Betsy Wetsies were living together because it was wartime and our husands were off fighting. Then we'd get a telegram saying our husbands had been blown to smithereens, which meant the two of us could live together forever if we wanted. Well, that's what it felt like now. We cruised around town, Jase and Amelia singing the ABC song over and over till we finally yelled, "Shut up, you little rodents!" then they bounced around the car laughing and bumping their heads on the ceiling, until they settled into their customary positions: heads out windows like dogs. Meanwhile, Fay and I hunted for wildflowers, which we picked by the bucketful, and cute guys, mostly in sports cars. When we saw one of them approaching, we'd say, "Wave, kids!" which they did like windup dolls.

Then it was dusk of a paralyzingly hot day. We'd just gotten ice cream cones for the kids and were driving around a part of town that was strange to us, the part of town where great aluminum sheds loomed near factories with smokestacks, at ends of streets with old shingled houses and forlorn-looking bushes. And there, in the distance, we saw a cluster of those same sports cars parked by a ballpark.

We recognized a couple of guys. They were on the Italian Club team, which was playing the Elks team. The Italian Club guys wore jeans. Bandanna headbands dammed the sweat on their foreheads and kept their long hair out of their faces. They smoked cigarettes in the outfield and clenched them between their teeth to make catches. They pranced around the bases instead of running when they hit homers. Some of these guys were the same boys who drove by me and Donna when we had sat under the tree, sticking our chins in the air, waiting for Denny Winters. I knew their names from my brother's yearbooks. They were older than us by three or four years. They were the type of gone-by hoods who stole hubcaps and had fights with chains and bricks in high school. Only now they were hippies. "Far out," I said to Fay. "Groovy," Fay said to me.

After that, the Italian Club bar was our hangout. It was the same room where Raymond had gotten drunk on Seagram's 7s at our wedding. The room was big and dark like the belly of a whale. The bar was mahogany, and lined with guys called Rat and Indian, Chip and Skip, Buzzard and Deacon. Half of them were married and thought nothing of the fact that they were drinking at a bar every night. If their wives called looking for them, automatically the bartender said, "Haven't seen him." If they talked about their wives at all, it was as though they were aliens, who flushed their pot down toilets and had fits when they showed up drunk at dawn, then wouldn't talk or have sex for days after.

"What," I asked, "do you think gives you the right to drink at bars and have all the fun you want while your wife is stuck home with kids?"

"Hey, Hank, hit me."

"Aren't you going to answer?"

"Maybe, maybe not. Why don't you put a bra on? You ever think your tits are going to end up at your waist by the time you're thirty?"

"Like your balls'll end up at your knees?"

"Hey, you're all right. I like you."

I'd read Betty Friedan, Germaine Greer, and Simone de Beauvoir, and I was ready, I was willing, I was chomping at the bit to personally fight for the rights of all women, with the help of my best friend and fellow victim, Fay. Since they wouldn't listen when we talked, we took action.

On our list, we made columns headed: name, age, astrological sign, penis size, and performance, rated one to ten. Then we dressed up in our hiphugger jeans and skimpy jerseys that left our belly buttons exposed and strutted into the club to lure men home (never the married ones) to lay, fuck, hump, ball, screw—that's the way we talked to amuse each other—and dispense with any nuance of love or romance. We got right to the point, which was to say, "Do you want to fuck?" If ever some guy had the audacity to try to light our cigarettes, say, we jumped all over him. "What do we look like, damsels in distress?"

Which in a way we were, because soon after we'd found the club, Fay's creep of an ex-husband sneaked up in the night and stole back the yellow Dodge, leaving us carless and furious—because it had been men who'd knocked us up, men who'd left us with kids, and men who got the cars.

The night of Beatrice's picnic, Fay and I were hoping we could get our mothers or Trudy our neighbor to take the kids so we could hitch to the club and pick up some guys, or at the very least have some drinks to take the edge off the acid. Which at the moment was making my ears fill with static. Jason had taken to burying me with grass and was almost finished. He was talking to himself in a murmur, "All I have left are her feet," he said. "The toes are the hardest. . . ."

Amelia ran up. "What're you doing?" she said.

"Burying my mother."

"Can I?"

"All right. When we're done, we have to find a flower. We can stick it in her mouth so it'll stand up."

"That's enough," I said, sitting up.

"*Maaaa!*" Jason yelled.

"What do you want? You were making me dead."

"Let's do it to my mother," Amelia suggested.

"Okay," Jase said, then he and Amelia ran off.

I felt abandoned, adrift, without Jason's anchoring me down. I watched him and Amelia run across the lawn to Fay. They bumped shoulders and ran at exactly the same speed. Jason was six months older, but they were constantly mistaken for twins. Jason was the type who liked to go first and win, and Amelia let him. They got along as well as their mothers did. They slept in Jason's room and got up together every morning before me and Fay, poured each other cereal, and ate it in front of the TV while watching cartoons. Fay and I slept in my room across the hall, but whenever one of us invited a man to sleep over, the other one slept on the couch and told the kids they couldn't watch television. Then they sat in the kitchen and chatted like chipmunks or went out earlier than usual.

When I had a guy over and at some point of the morning we appeared in the kitchen, Amelia flirted with him, while Jason suddenly forgot how to do everything, like put on his own sweater or pour his own milk or talk if asked a direct question by anyone but me. As I'd always figured, Fay lucked out having a girl, because girls didn't have a male territorial thing about boyfriends.

Jase had laid a bombshell on me the last time I had a

guy stay over. The guy had left and I was talking to Jase in a pretend foreign language to get him mad. I don't know why—maybe because he was the wrong sex. Finally, he stood up, red in the face, and yelled, "Stop!" I was shocked. Jason hardly ever lost his temper. I burst out laughing, then he looked like he might cry, so I said, "What's the matter? I was just asking you what you want to be when you grow up, and you wouldn't answer."

"You were talking stupid."

"I know. Sorry. But answer me. What do you want to be?"

"A cop."

"A pig! What do you want to be a pig for?"

"So I can shoot people."

This coming from a kid who never had a toy gun in his life? This coming from a kid who'd been taught, make peace not war? Then the obvious dawned on me. "You want to be one because Pop is."

"No sir."

"Jason, if you become a cop, I'll disown you."

"What's disown mean?"

"It means I'll never talk to you and you can't come in my house anymore."

"Don't say that." Now he looked like he was going to cry again.

Then I remembered reverse psychology. "Go ahead. I don't care. If you want to be a cop, be a cop."

As I watched him and Amelia at the far end of the lawn reaching into a bag of marshmallows Beatrice was holding, I began to dream, one of my favorites: What would my life be without Jason? I'd be living in New York City, appearing in a play. Probably *Hair*. One night John Lennon would show up without Yoko and we'd go out for drinks. Then I axed the fantasy. I tried to Be Here Now and think of the good things about being a mother. I couldn't think of one good thing. Not one. What I thought of was Lenny LaRoyce and his bus. Fay and I'd gone to high school with Lenny, and when he got out of the service, he converted a school bus and drove it across country. When he returned recently, he parked his bus on his friend's lawn for a couple of months and began dropping by the club. Fay seduced him. Then one night he invited Fay and Amelia and Jase and me to sleep on the bus. Wouldn't you know the couple in the bunk above Jase and me would have to get hyperactive in the middle of the night and start humping and bumping and moaning and groaning to beat the band? Jason woke up and said, "Ma, what're they doing?"

"Having sex," I said.

"What's sex?" he said.

I'd told Jason the facts of life since the day he was born practically, because I believed sex was a natural part of life and nothing to be ashamed of. But he never remembered. It wasn't the time to repeat the whole thing again, so I said, "Sh, go to sleep."

When Lenny invited me and Fay to go on his next trip and to bring our kids, I seriously considered it. But then I thought, Oh right, and then I'd have that feeling of guilt, like I was doing the wron thing, whenever Jase woke up in the night hearing people screwing.

I watched him sticking up his face and hands with marshmallow and thought I should tell him he's had enough, but who wanted to listen to him whine? Fay walked over then, sat next to me on the grass, and watched the party from a distance with me: Beatrice and her nine-to-five friends eating hot dogs in bikinis. Finally, she said, "Let's blow this stupid picnic," which was exactly my sentiment.

Of course, Amelia and Jase had a fit because of the marshmallows, but our timing was right, because a minute after we stepped onto the road, we got a ride home.

We found no one to baby-sit that night, so after the kids fell asleep, we sat on the front stoop and tried to will some guys to our house. I was thinking specifically about Hal, the bartender, who hurt my feelings because he gave me drinks on the house and let himself be seduced but had never once called or even spent the day with me after a night together. The last time he'd dropped me off in the morning, he'd said, "You're hostile, you know that? You think you're Janis Joplin. You'd better get it while you can. What do you think's going to happen when your good looks fade?" Then he'd reached over and opened the door for me to get out. He said, "Better make hay while the sun shines," as he backed out of the driveway. This struck me as mean, which was probably why I liked the guy to begin with.

Now Fay said, "The only time they come by is when they know we have drugs."

"All we ever do is talk about guys, think about guys, and go to the club to look for guys," I said. "How can we call ourselves liberated?"

"We do what we want and we don't take shit."

"We need money," I said.

"I'll be rich one day," Fay said. "Then I'm coming back in a red Ferrari."

"We could go to the club. They'd all want to drive it, but we wouldn't let them."

"I would."

"I wouldn't. I think I hate men more than you do. Maybe it's because you had two brothers."

"You had a brother."

"Come on. He was the only son in an Italian family, plus, we never talked."

"That's my problem with this women's lib shit. I'd rather hang out with men than women. Face it. Women are boring. All girls talk about are their babies, their husbands, or their boyfriends, or the fucking sale at some stupid store. Look at Beatrice. Pastel *pantsuits*. Her makeup in a goddamn tackle box. Fucking push-up bras. And she thinks we're crazy? Most women are dumb."

"That's only in Wallingford. And they're not stupid, just unliberated."

"That's what you think. They're worse in Pennsylvania."

"I disagree."

She took my cigarette and dragged from it. "Well, I think we're alike anyhow. We're both tactless. I couldn't believe when you said to Beatrice, 'Nice bathing suit. It matches your skin.' Her bathing suit was fucking *orange*."

"I didn't even think it was rude. I guess it was."

"That's what I mean."

The next morning, we didn't talk. We took our last two hits of speed and set to cleaning the house. Fay took the kitchen and the bathroom. I took the living room and the bedrooms. After a couple of hours I heard the kettle whistling in the kitchen and sat down at the table for a break. Fay had finished the kitchen. The counters were bare and shiny and the emerald-green floor looked like it was covered with ice. She'd picked bright yellow flowers for the table, and by the end of the day there'd be flowers in every room, including on the tank of the toilet. As I sipped my tea—from a cup Fay always made sure had a saucer beneath it—I thought how much better life was now that Fay was my roommate. I watched her take the cellophane off my Kools and crinkle it in her fingers, which moved like spiders' legs. I felt like I was studying a person who was alone. She bit the inside of her lip and began forming the cellophane into a sculpture of a discus thrower. Fay was a great artist. Back in high school, when the art teacher asked her to paint a Santa on the glass ramp between two buildings, she painted him giving the finger. When the teacher told her to go erase it, she erased everything but the hand with the finger, and got two weeks' detention.

Fay was only five feet tall, and everything about her was miniature, except her hair, which was like a lion's mane. It was in two thick and long pigtails that stuck out from the sides of her head and draped over the tops of her arms to her elbows. I thought she was beautiful. She thought I was too. She said I had a classic Roman nose and an interestingly angular face. She'd done several sketches of me during our evenings alone. She said she would make a painting one day when she could afford oils. She said she'd call it Beverly. I wondered how long living together would last. I supposed it would end as soon as one of us fell in love. Maybe that's why we always made fun of each other's men, because each of us was afraid the other would get too attached. Fay got up and put Carole King on the stereo. I wondered if she thought about me whenever she heard "You've Got a Friend," the way I thought about her. I sat back, closed my eyes, and realized I was actually happy.

We'd made a deal with Lenny for that night. He'd use our house to sell eleven pounds of marijuana, because his bus was being watched by the police, and we'd get an ounce of pot for our trouble. Since Fay and

Lenny had to stay home to sell the pot anyway, Fay would baby-sit for Jason while I went on a date with this guy named Brad I saw sometimes, even though Amelia was spending the night at her grandmother's.

I was probably shooting at cans in the moonlight with Brad's .38 when Fay and Lenny and the buyer, who Fay said had a long ponytail and smoked incense-smelling cigarettes, were weighing pounds of pot in my kitchen, and Fay noticed the Uglies on the front stoop. Without thinking twice, she did what we always did: positioned the stereo speakers in front of the screen door to drive them off. This was in retaliation for their forbidding Jase and Amelia to play on their side of the yard, because we sometimes let them run nude in the neighborhood.

This time the Uglies called the police, who appeared at the front door. When Fay answered it, she slammed the door in their faces and said, "We're fucked. It's the pigs."

When I returned home in Brad's pickup truck, three cop cars were crisscrossed on the lawn, their red lights spinning and bouncing off houses. "Turn around," I said, feeling a lump like an apple in the middle of my chest.

We went directly to a bar. "Let's book," Brad said. "I got this buddy on a commune in Colorado."

"With what money?"

"I got five hundred in the bank."

"No strings? If we were just friends, that would be cool?"

"Cool." He nodded.

I looked at him then and knew for certain the only reason I was with him was because when I squinted, he looked like John Lennon. "If I left, after seven years I could get clemency and come back?"

"I don't know. Sure. I think so."

Jason would be ten. The fifth grade. Maybe my parents would've destroyed my pictures and never mentioned my name. Then, when I surprised him in the playground, he'd look at me as if to say, And who the hell are you? When I said, "I'm your mother," he'd say, "She's dead."

I went home to get arrested.

CHAPTER 9

WHEN I walked into my
house, Lieutenant O'Reilly, my father's best friend,
said, "Have a nice ride with your boyfriend? We figured
you'd be back." He was showing off. This was
supposed to make me think he was Svengali.

I sat down at the kitchen table where O'Reilly indicated
as though it were his house. Cops were ripping
the purple, blue, and magenta slipcovers off the furniture
in the living room; they were flipping through
books and throwing them on the floor; they were
opening jars in my refrigerator. Then his sidekick, another
plainclothesman, Detective Beaumont, started
shaking every pill bottle in the house in front of my
face. "Sunshine? Windowpane? Speed? THC?" I knew
he was trying to impress me with his knowledge of
names, which made me think he was a jerk, which
made me less afraid. "Vitamins, aspirin, Midol," I
said. It was a good thing I took that last hit of speed
for housecleaning.

"You may as well come clean," O'Reilly said.
"We're sending them to the lab in the morning anyway."

"Waste your money," I shrugged.

"You don't seem to understand the trouble you're
in. We found eleven pounds of marijuana in your

house, miss. That's intent to sell, a felony. Your father was here. He was very upset. We told him to go home. He took your son with him."

I looked at my hands on my lap. They were so tanned from hitchhiking in the sun all summer, my nails looked white.

"You got anything to say for yourself?"

I sat on my hands and said nothing.

"All right." O'Reilly stood up. "Bring her downtown. We're gonna book her."

I saw neighbors in the windows across the street watching as I rode off in the backseat of a police car.

At the station, Beaumont dragged my arms beneath spotlights and said, "No tracks. Must be skin popping, huh?" I took pride in never touching heroin or sticking a needle in my body, and his accusation made me furious. But I figured that's what he wanted, so I acted nonchalant. He fingerprinted and mug-shot me, then deposited me across a desk from O'Reilly. I examined the ink on my fingertips while O'Reilly laid into me. "We gave you leeway," he said. "We gave you a chance, for your father. We've had ten loud-music complaints, but we ignored them, hoping you'd straighten your act. You just didn't know when to give up. Your father says, Throw the book at her. He's fed up."

I kept thinking of the time O'Reilly and his wife had come to pick up my parents to go out dancing. His wife had huge breasts that were barely concealed by her low-cut dress. I was having a pajama party with six of my friends and we all walked into the kitchen one by one to get a glass of water and a gander at Mrs. O'Reilly. The next morning, my mother said, "We knew what you were doing. It wasn't very nice."

"Well, miss," O'Reilly said. "Your ass is fried now.

Next time we see a car parked in your driveway overnight, the door's coming off and you're busted for
prostitution."

I should've known. It wasn't the drugs, it was sex.

They locked me in a cell. Fay was in the one next
door. "Do you believe this?" she said.

"No," I said.

She started giggling.

"I can't laugh," I said.

"One day you'll think it's a riot. I picked my nose
and stuck the booger on the wall."

I wished I had her spirit.

My parents didn't bail me out. Some of Lenny's
friends did. When Fay got out she went with her
mother, who'd bailed her out.

All of the houses were dark on the court, except
mine, which was lit like a birthday cake. The doors
were flung open, and the inside looked like a hurricane
hit it. The cops had left the cushion covers lying on the
floor. Every can and pan and vitamin pill was spilled
from my cupboards onto my counters and floors. My
bedroom was the most upsetting. The contents of the
drawers were dumped into a heap on my bed, with my
bikini underwear and my diaphragm on top. Our
"Love the One You're With" poster had been torn
from the wall and ripped to shreds.

Fay had told me back in jail that my father had
gone nuts and torn up the poster. After he did that, his
buddies advised him to go home. Which he did, but
not before he confiscated Jason.

The next morning, when I walked into my parents'
house to reclaim my son, my father was weeping at the
table again. I didn't sit down. My mother, the lioness
when her husband was hurt, stood up. "Well, you've
had your fun. Now you're going to pay the price.

What'd you think, you could just do whatever you want and get away with it? I thought you were the one who's supposed to be so smart. You're killing your father. You put every gray hair on that poor man's head."

"Where's Jason?" I said.

"Never mind where Jason is," my father said. He blew his nose and looked out the window. "*Now* you think about him." He wiped his eyes and stuffed his hankie in his back pocket. Then he looked at me. "You mark my words. You get in trouble again, the first complaint, I'm filing for custody. You'll lose him. I'll have you declared an unfit mother. You think I'm kidding? Just try me."

An unfit mother? I wanted to scream. *And you call yourself a fit father?* You never even knew how old I was on my birthdays. But I knew from a lifetime of experience that if I uttered one word in response to an accusation leveled by the big man, the boss and the king, I was "answering back," which was just cause for a slap across the face.

So I stood there and looked contrite. I guess my look made him sick, because he walked out of the room.

Next, I expected my mother to go get the Bible and make me swear on it never to do another bad thing. But she said, "What did you think when you were in jail?"

"Nothing," I said.

"You got a beautiful son. I don't know why you can't be happy with that."

"There are other things in the world, Ma, besides being a mother."

"Like what? Getting drunk? Having boyfriends?"

"Like fun," I said. I could've said, Like an education, a career, travel, experience, but I would've started crying.

My sister Rose, now twelve, walked into the kitchen and smiled at me like she felt sorry. She sat down at the table. Next my other sister, Phyllis, now seventeen, walked in and made her mouth clench and go crooked as if to say, This is so stupid. She sat next to Rose and across from me. Phyllis was running for secretary of the senior class. I wondered if she'd lose if my arrest made the paper.

"Where's Jason?" I said.

"Watching *Mighty Heroes,*" Phyllis said.

"I wanted to watch *Lucy,* but I lost the flip," Rose said.

"Oh, you," my mother said. "You're the older. You should tell him. You're such a softy."

"Hi, Ma," Jase said as he turned the corner into the hall from the living room.

"Hi, son," I said.

He sat on my lap. "Could I get a GI Joe?" he said.

In this way, I knew that he'd interpreted getting plucked from his bed and carried through a house of marauding cops as my having done something I should feel sorry for. Because he was trying to get a payment, a reward. And not just any reward. He was asking for something he knew I'd never buy him in a million years. Maybe he thought GI Joe was like his father.

"What do you want one of those stupid things for?" Phyllis said.

"He wants it because everybody else does," Rose said.

"No sir," he said.

"Leave the kid alone," my mother said. "I don't know why he can't have a GI Joe."

"Because toys like that encourage violence," I said.

"It's just a doll," she said, not listening.

"It's just drugs. It's just sex," I said into the table.

"What?" she said.

My sisters giggled.

"Ma!" Jase said, and slapped my hand.

CHAPTER 10

THIS is what I wondered as I waited for my trial date: Why did my parents decide to name their first daughter Beverly Ann Donofrio and forever brand me with the initials B.A.D.? What did they think? I mean, as a kid those initials were a heavy burden. That word carries a lot of weight when you've just come off being a baby. "No, no. *Bad* girl."

In the second grade, my teacher made us put our initials in bold letters on the face of a folder we'd store our artwork in all year. Every time I pulled that huge manila thing from my cubby, somebody pointed and jeered, "Beverly's bad." Then the rest of them chimed in, "Bad Beverly, bad Beverly." To a normal second grader, it could be rough. To a hypersensitive little girl such as I was, it was devastating. I mean, I was the type of kid who cried every time I saw a kitten without its mother. And I was dainty. I freaked out if I got dirt on my hands or water on my feet. Until I was four, I refused to set foot off the porch without a babushka because I was convinced that birds would dive-bomb me and yank out all my hair. Come to think of it, maybe my parents should've named me Catherine Rose Ann Zelda Yolanda.

Now, at the age of twenty-one, with my name spelled out in the newspaper, which called me a member of an alleged drug ring caught with ten thousand dollars' worth of marijuana (the asking price was actually a thousand dollars), you not only could've called me *bad* and *crazy* but notorious.

First thing, the public-housing authority threatened to evict me if I didn't kick Fay out. So one windy Saturday, I helped her load her stuff into a van and we hugged goodbye in the driveway. She was only going to her mother's, but it felt like the other end of the world. When we pulled out of the embrace, her hair was flying all over her face and whipping against mine. Tears came to my eyes, but I don't think she noticed. She and Amelia climbed into the van. Jason held my hand. Fay rolled down the window and said, "Do you believe this shit?" then started to laugh. As she backed down the drive, she said, "Hey, Bev," shot the finger to Backes Court, and said, "Fuck'm." For my part, I have to admit, I didn't think it was all that funny.

I walked into the house with Jason. It was empty now, except for Jason's old crib mattress shoved into a corner of the living room and a white-topped table in the kitchen that Fay's mother had given me out of the goodness of her heart.

I sat on the mattress. Jason sat next to me. "Why do they have to go?" he said.

"Because I got arrested for something I didn't do."

"Why?"

"Because life's not fair." He was only three and a half but I wanted to give it to him straight, so he wouldn't be the type of kid I was. We're talking warped. I used to fling myself on the ground, bury my face in the grass, and kiss dirt because I loved America that much. If some kid told me to get out of his yard, I jammed my hands on my hips and wouldn't budge an inch. "It's a free country," I said. What an idiot.

I still hadn't changed as much as I thought though, because come the spring of 1972, I expected my trial to be like TV: my lawyer as clever as Perry Mason, as nice as Fred MacMurray. He'd foil the police with a technicality like illegal entry or coercion or inadmissible evidence, and I'd be off scot-free.

But I didn't get to meet the guy until five minutes before court. He was short, ugly, and a man of few words. Nineteen to be exact: "We can make a deal. I'll ask for a suspended sentence plus probation."

"It wasn't my pot," I said.

"It's the best I can do."

Then the prosecutor said to the judge, "We recommend a six months' suspended sentence and two years' probation."

The judge scowled, ran a hand through his hair, shook his head, and said, "Humph. A mother on welfare, using public funds to buy drugs. I'm not inclined to go easy on you, but there is the child to consider," and gave me exactly what the lawyers asked for.

Which translated into a visit every Wednesday with Mr. Stanley Stupski, Wallingford's crack probation officer. I sat on a bench in the town hall while Jason slid around the shiny floor playing with his Matchbox cars. Sometimes my father walked by. Then Jason stood up on his knees and said, "Hi, Pop." My father mussed his hair and winked at me. Which I appreciated. After all, he was probably embarrassed. I was his daughter and I was sitting on the same bench with every other derelict in town, some of whom he'd no doubt busted.

Sooner or later, Stan the man appeared in his doorway, pointed at me, said, "Bouchard," then stabbed his thumb at his office. I squeezed past his beer belly, pulling Jason in behind me, then lifted him to my lap like a shield.

"So, been to any pot parties lately? Orgies maybe?" Stan began the session.

"That's disgusting," I replied.

"What? I thought that's what all you hippies are into. You'd tell me if you knew about any, wouldn't you?"

I rolled my eyes and looked out the window.

"You got anything to say to me?"

"No."

"You got a bad attitude. That's your problem. Now, if you came in here and acted civilized, said, 'Hello, Mr. Stupski, how are you?' I might treat you better. Maybe you'd come in every other week. Once a month. I'd say, Now, here's a nice girl. I think I'll give her a break. But you act like a snot. Didn't anybody ever teach you you win more friends with sugar than vinegar?"

"No," I said truthfully.

By the summer, Fay had deserted me to move to Minneapolis with her new boyfriend, who was a graduate student in psychology. After a couple of months, she wrote me that Amelia was in a Head Start program and by the New Year of 1973, she would be enrolled in college, which her older brother was going to pay for. I was jealous. Wallingford had no Head Start, and obviously, college was out of the question for me. My older brother wasn't going to pay for anything. In fact, my older brother had just made a return appearance in town from four years in the navy, where he'd been in a top-security position, and now would tell no one where he'd been, what he'd done, or where he got what looked like a bullet wound in the muscle behind his left shin. As soon as he got home, the chair at the dinner table, the one at the other head of the table from my father—the chair I'd been sitting in every time I ate over for four years—reverted to him and I retreated to the sidelines with my mother, sisters, and Jason. Come to think of it, I'm surprised Jason, being of the master sex, hadn't gotten the seat across from my father all those years. And guess what profession my brother chose after the service: *cop*. He hadn't been on the force more than a few months before he was written up in the paper as a hero. He'd been on the beat when he spotted a car careening crazily around a corner, then screeching away as fast as the wind. My brother heard a siren in the distance and figured the car was being pursued, so acting on instinct, he dropped onto one knee, aimed his pistol, and shot at the runaway car's tires, which went flat. It was rumored he would probably get the cop-of-the-year award for his action, while I thought he should've been suspended for reckless endangerment of the citizens who'd been all over the sidewalks, going to the post office or the bank. What if one of those bullets richocheted off the asphalt and into one of them?

In any case, there was my older brother, the prince to my father's king, being Mr. Good Citizen again while I was being a nothing, trapped with a kid. I decided that even if I couldn't go to college, I would educate myself. I'd pick authors then read every book he or she had written and then I'd read their biographies. I figured maybe I could be a writer too. I still wrote an occasional poem, but now I would switch to prose to make money. That was the real beauty. I wouldn't need a car or a baby-sitter. I could make money and do it from home. Exactly one year after I got busted, I wrote a story and applied to the Famous Writers School. I tried for irony. It was about a girl in the fifth grade who got the hiccups when she went to confession and they wouldn't stop. For days, weeks, months, whenever she opened her mouth, she had a hiccup attack. Since they started in confession, of course she thought it was the wrath of God, so she bent over backward acting like a saint. But then one day, out of habit she lies to her mother and the hiccups miraculously stop. They gave me a B and said I had talent but needed instruction—for a price. What a dope. I never considered the cost, or maybe I just thought I'd get an A and they'd beg me to be their student, or maybe I'd get discovered by a famous writer. After the disappointment had time to sink in, I got real and went to an employment agency.

The counselor, Mr. Kelly, told me not to expect much. I had no skills or experience, but he'd see what he could do. He called at the end of the week. He had a job as a clerk for a little over minimum wage at Cyanamid, the plastics plant that fumigated Wallingford with noxious chemical stink. He told me to get a pen and jot down the time, the date, and the office number. Then he said, "There's just one more thing. I'd like you to wear a bra. It makes a better impression."

I hung up the phone and heard my ears drumming. I was shocked that I was so shocked. I'd never give that guy the time of day after he'd said that. How could he possibly think it was any of his business whether I wore a bra or not? And if that's the way jobs were, if you had to wear a bra to get one, I'd rather stay poor, unemployed, and true to my principles, thank you. With no car and no one to care for Jason (my mother worked every night at a factory now and I couldn't ask her), the job had been a pipe dream anyway. It all boiled down to the same old thing: the trouble I'd gotten myself into having sex with a hood in high school. And the name of the trouble was Jason. My jailer.

I read him stories every night, to encourage a love of reading early on. That way he might go to college and not end up like his mother or, worse, his father. He played mostly with three foul-mouthed sisters from across the road, who bit their mother, Trudy, to get her attention, but luckily they didn't seem to be rubbing off. His favorite thing in the world was to go to the brook, catch a couple of frogs, then keep them in a coffee can in his room. When he'd do this, I'd hear the thump thump thump of frogs hitting their heads against the plastic lid. This went on all night, until I woke up in the morning screaming, "Let the goddamn frogs out!" He begged me to take him fishing, because he dreamed of catching a good one-footer and keeping it in the bathtub. What was it with boys and the way they liked to imprison other creatures?

Jase was beautiful to look at, knew his please-and-thank yous, liked to kiss and hug and cuddle, but still he was like an alien creature. I still wished he was a girl. Even so—boy, jailer, bane of my life—he was my main companion.

We went to my mother's nearly every day for dinner. I watched soaps with my sisters when they came home from school while Jase hung out with my mother in the kitchen. He colored and played with Lincoln Logs or his remote-control car, then when dinner was served, if he didn't like what my mother made for everyone else, she made him something special, treatment that previously only my father had received. Occasionally, I borrowed my mother's car to ride with Jase around the countryside, which usually ended with a visit to the Friendly Cows. As soon as we pulled up, they came sauntering from their shed to the barbed wire. They slobbered our hands with wet noses. We gave them names and fed them fistfuls of grass. I felt an affinity with the Friendly Cows, and so did Jason. When we left, he always said, "Poor cows." It killed me they were earmarked for slaughter. Neither Jason nor I liked to eat beef during this period. At night, sometimes I told Jason stories about the Friendly Cows, in which the Cows went through all sorts of hardships and misadventures but ended up happy in India, where they were sacred.

But the monotony of my life was about to end, I thought. It was the fall of 1973 and Jason's first day of kindergarten. I'd have half of every day free, kidless, by myself, alone—a state I'd been looking forward to since the day he was born. The next year, when he was gone all day, maybe, just maybe, I could get a job and join the world. I dressed him in gray boy pants, the type with a belt instead of a stretchy waistband. Then I pulled a light blue jersey over his head, to bring out the blue in his eyes. He was a beauty. I knew the teacher would love him. Most women did.

I'd borrowed my mother's car for the occasion. The kindergarten room was plastered with the ABCs, pictures of animals, domestic and wild, and chaotic with mothers and kids. I thought the other mothers were staring at me because I was too young to have a kid in kindergarten, but then I thought people stared at me everywhere I went since the day my name appeared in the paper.

We stood in line for our turn with the teacher, who wore a bright red skirt, a white blouse with a Peter Pan collar, and had translucent skin like a nun's. One second, I wished I hadn't worn my jeans, and the next, I was glad I'd been true to myself and dressed natural.

Jason squeezed my hand tighter and leaned his head into my waist. "You scared?" I asked.

He nodded.

"What of?" I said.

"I don't know."

Half the time, Jason was afflicted with the Donofrio male habit of noncommunication. So I helped him out. "I was afraid when I went to kindergarten," I said.

"You were?"

"Everybody is."

"Why?"

"I don't know. I guess you're afraid to leave your mother. Afraid of all the strange kids. Just afraid because you don't know what's going to happen next. Right?"

He nodded his head and relaxed his grip on my hand. "Well, I'm not going anywhere; some of the kids you'll like and some you won't; and school will get to be such a routine so fast you'll wish you didn't know what's happening next."

"Mm-hm." Jason believed everything I said, because I always told him the truth. Then he added, "You'll pick me up, right?" He had to check.

"Right."

Mrs. Deerie, the teacher, stuck a name tag on Jason—"So I can learn your name, young man"—then pointed him to a chair at a large square table. Jason sat down and stared straight ahead. "Well, Jase," I said. "I guess I'll be going."

He nodded and kept staring.

"Don't I get a kiss?"

He stood up and kissed me quickly, then sat back down and took the same position.

Back home, I drank a cup of coffee. The birds outside the window seemed louder, seemed to make a hysterical racket, because the neighborhood was so silent. I envied Jason and all the kids. First days of school were exciting. My mind crowded with pictures of Jason's beginning: playing ring-around-the-rosy, eating a graham cracker and drinking milk through a straw at snack time. The teacher telling some kid, who definitely would not be Jason, to stop blowing bubbles. While I imagined him learning to raise his hand to ask permission to go to the bathroom, I knocked my coffee off the table. It broke, and I cried. And do you know what I thought? Not, What will I do without Jason. Not, I wish I could go to school too. But, I must be getting my period; I can't wait till menopause.

I was depressed that autumn, and it didn't help that Jason's teacher thought I was a faulty mother. First, at Halloween, I poured green food dye into white baby shoe polish and painted Jason's skin to make him a green Martian. I thought it showed imagination. But when he came home, his face was washed clean. He said, "Mrs. Deerie said it was poison."

Then, at my first parent-teacher conference, she said, "I'm concerned about your son. Whenever there's a little roughhousing, you know the way boys do, Jason retreats to a puzzle or off with the girls. Is there a man in his life?"

"No," I said.

"Nobody to throw around a football or play catch?"

"Well, my father, but . . ."

I could tell she thought me pathetic and Jason's life impoverished because I couldn't provide him with the essentials. I figured her assessment of me was on target.

A month later, after Jason had been bugging me

and bugging me, "I want a butch, I want a butch" (I guess to look like every other little redneck in town), I took out my electric razor, purchased with S&H green stamps, and buzzed off his beautiful hair. Problem was, it came off in patches that made his skull look like a map of the United States, so I had to shave him bald. The kids called him Bald Eagle at the bus stop. They said, "Snatch a pebble from my hand, Grasshopper," from a kung fu TV show that featured a bald guy. This never failed to make Jason shoot me a dirty look.

I was standing at the bus stop with him, because I'd volunteered to work in the school library to have something to do. I rode the bus with him two days a week and Jase didn't seem the least bit embarrassed to sit next to his mother—I guess, because he didn't think of me so much as a mother as another kid growing up. On the ride, I indicated other kids and asked if he liked them, to which he usually answered yes. At his school, I pretended I was a real librarian as I put books back on the shelves in alphabetical order and recommended *Horton the Elephant* or *The Phantom Tollbooth* to kids who came in with a pass.

Then one freezing November day, Jason's teacher was on duty when we disembarked the bus. She took me aside and said in a whisper, "I was wondering. Did Jason have lice?"

"No," I said. "He wanted a butch and I went too far."

"I see," she said, not seeing.

Then she wrapped her arm around Jason's shoulder, bent to his height, and said, "So, how are you today, my little helper? Do me a favor, dear. Put my pocketbook in my desk, will you? Well, back to work," she said, dismissing me.

She thought I was a miserable mother and that she

cared more for my son than I did. Maybe it was true. I'd been dating a schoolteacher who wouldn't park his car in my driveway because he said he might end up fired. He pretended I didn't have a kid. And so did I. So whenever we went out, I never invited Jason. One time, it was a Sunday, we were driving down Main Street and I saw my parents in their car with Jason, coming from the opposite direction. When we passed, I looked out the rear window and saw Jason looking out the rear window too. He kept looking, and then he was too far away for me to tell. I'd felt sad then, and in the library that day, thinking about it, I felt sad again. I couldn't concentrate. I stamped *received* when I should've stamped *date due*. I rested my elbow on the stamp pad and ruined forever my favorite shirt. Then there was the kicker.

The teacher across the hall was a screamer, and today was no exception. She said, "All right, class, attention, pay attention. . . . What's a factory?"

No response.

Louder: "What . . . is . . . a . . . factory?"

No response.

Screaming: *"Where do your parents work?"*

That did it. I ran into the bathroom to start crying. Factory work was all I could hope for, and maybe it would be all my son would hope for too. I was a white-trash person who shaved my son's hair. I might as well be living in West Virginia. Who was I kidding, pretending to be a librarian? People like Jason's teacher thought I was an idiot. I cried so hard the janitor knocked on the door to ask what was the matter. Finally, I controlled myself. When we got home, I called my mother and said I was sick. She volunteered to take Jason overnight and bring him to school the next morning.

As soon as he left, I called the hospital and asked for the emergency room. I said to the man who answered, "If someone took a hundred aspirins, would they die?" He said one hundred aspirins could eat out the wall of his stomach, which would make him hemorrhage and die. He said I should most certainly bring him in. Then he asked who was calling, and I hung up. Next, I carried my bottle of one hundred aspirins along with two glasses of water to my room, emptied the pills onto my bed, and took two and two and two. Probably, it would be my mother and Jase who'd find me. Probably, when she dropped him off after school the next day, they'd call for me, and when I didn't answer, she'd send Jase up to see if I was sleeping. Maybe I'd leave a note on the table so Jason wouldn't have to see me dead. But what could I say? Dear Mom and Jason and Rose and Phyllis and Dad and Mike, forgive me for offing myself, Love, Bev?

I took two more, and lines like "It's always darkest before the dawn" and "When winter comes, can spring be far behind?" came to mind. I didn't believe them. I took two more.

Pregnant at seventeen Divorced at nineteen. Arrested at twenty-one. Killed myself at twenty-three. There was a beautiful symmetry. I took two more.

I didn't like my destiny. God had it in for me. I didn't believe in him anyway, but still I said, "Oh God," or "Please, dear God," or "God help me." I promised myself to never again ever mention his name. But what was I thinking? I'd be dead. I took two more. That made fourteen.

The first time it occurred to me there might not be a God, I was twelve and had just discovered Hamlet's soliloquy. I couldn't sleep that night. A mulberry branch beat on my window while Mr. Gerace played

"Taps" over and over in his backyard. He must've been drunk, because it was late. I had closed my eyes and tried to imagine myself dead—what it would be like, to be dust, no memory, nothing. I'd decided even then it could be bliss. Now, I took two more.

Jason would be better off, no question. Even if he did have to live with my smothering mother and mean father. At least my father wasn't mean to him. Not yet. But wait till the kid reached high school and got caught sneaking a beer. Don't think about it. I took two more.

My formerly beautiful son looked like a concentration-camp victim. I took two more. And two more. That made twenty-two.

Then I remembered my first suicide attempt. I'd been thirteen and in love with Trevis Glasker, who was sixteen and lived around the block. He wore sunglasses, said his name was Ray and that he was blind. I made a fool of myself mooning over him and yelling at his friends when they made fun of his condition. Then one day Ray walked up, took off his sunglasses, said, "I can see you," and started laughing. His blindness had been a big joke that everyone was in on. I ran home wailing so loud birds flew off treetops. I took a razor from the medicine chest, then dove into my closet. I hugged my clothes and started singing "The End of the World." By the end of the song, I wanted to sing it over. I did and got so carried away with the drama, the razor slipped from my fingers and fell between two floorboards. I decided I didn't want to kill myself anymore. For years after that, whenever I thought about Trevis Glasker, my face got hot and I wished I could forget the incident forever.

But then, one day, it seemed funny.

If I didn't kill myself now, one day I'd probably

laugh: being a convicted criminal while my father *and* my brother were cops, riding a bus with a bunch of kindergarteners to get to a fake job, making Jason look like a victim of lice. Maybe one day we'd discover some pictures of him, looking like a little Gandhi, in a shoebox and we'd roll around laughing. What song should I sing now? "It's My Party and I'll Die if I Want To?"

I decided not to do it.

CHAPTER 11

THERE'S definitely something to that darkest-before-the-dawn line because the next morning I called the psychiatric clinic at the hospital and my life started to look up. My social worker, Mrs. Goldfarb, took out a pad and a pencil and made a list of all the drugs I'd taken in my lifetime: LSD, mescaline, Percodan, horse tranquilizers, Seconal, cocaine, opium, amphetamines, hashish, and marijuana. She nodded her head and said, "That's quite an arsenal." When I told her about what a creep my probation officer had been, she was outraged. When I told her I felt guilty that Raymond became a junkie because I got pregnant and ruined his life, she told me that was ridiculous. When I told her I was afraid I didn't love Jason, she said she was sure I did. I appreciated her rage at Stanley Stupski, but I didn't believe her on the other two points. Still, it was great to have somebody on my side. Then after two months of once a week, she pronounced me an aesthete and said, "You're too intelligent to be wasting away. You should go to college."

I started crying.

She set up an interview for me at DVR, the division of vocational rehabilitation, where they'd give me a battery of tests: psychological, personality, aptitude, and achievement. If I scored crazy and smart enough, they'd send me to college; if I scored crazy and wasn't smart, I'd get vocational training.

DVR had been established after the Second World War to give veterans with physical disabilities some physical therapy and job training so they could join the work force. Then it was expanded to include everybody who was disabled, including psychologically or emotionally disturbed people, of which, obviously, I was one.

The day of the tests, I arrived at seven and was told to sit at a long metal table in a green room. Soon, a psychiatrist arrived. He wore wire-rim glasses and must've been seven feet tall and four feet wide. My strategy was to answer the questions like a crazy person so I'd be considered disabled and a candidate for college or training.

But it turned out I couldn't distinguish between crazy and sane, which made me think I really was a nut. First, there were the college board-type tests. Then the shrink asked me questions like, "What does the statement 'Shallow brooks make the most noise' mean?" I gave him figurative and literal. He looked impressed. He gave me inkblots. He gave me cartoon pictures to put in sequence. He gave me weird tests with questions like, "If you found a letter, addressed and stamped, lying on the ground, what would you do?" I figured to touch it would be a federal offense. Plus, towns don't have lost-and-founds. I knew that "Open it" was the wrong answer, although it sounded like something I'd do. "Mail it" never occurred to me. I said simply, "I don't know." Then he gave me pictures to make up stories about, and each time the psychiatrist held up a new one, it seemed there was only one story in the world that went with it.

In one picture there was a woman lying at the bottom of the stairs. Her eyes were closed, and an older woman was holding the young woman in her arms. I said, "The mistress of the house just fell down the stairs and broke her neck. She's dead. Now the maid's holding her and wondering if it was her fault because she put too much wax on the stairs. She's worried she'll get fired."

I probably should've said it was her mother and that the young woman just fainted or something, because a couple of weeks later, when I sat in the DVR counselor's cubicle to hear the results, the geriatric Mr. Randall lifted his feet onto a milk crate and said, "Our testing shows you're having a difficult time adjusting to adult life. You hate your mother." He blinked his eyes real fast and said, "Not unusual. Nothing you can't overcome. You have problems with your father, too. You buck against authority. Somebody tells you what to do, you do the opposite. If somebody told you to wear a bra, for example, you couldn't do it."

How did he know? And why do they all notice I'm not wearing one?

"You make it hard on yourself. It seems you also hate men. I understand. I can imagine it's not easy being a divorcee in this day and age. Men think they can take advantage."

They never stopped thinking about sex—even if they're about to croak in a minute like this one.

"You are very intelligent, I'm pleased to report." He leafed through the papers. "You scored in the ninety-seventh percentile of all freshmen entering college this year. That's quite high. The doctor was very excited. He recommends we send you to college."

I felt like Hester Prynne must've felt in the next chapter, the one that never got written, the one where she's in the woods on her way to the rest of her life and finally rips off that ridiculous *A* and throws it in the camp fire.

"No sense sending you to vocational training; you'd never be happy in a subordinate position. I can't see you going further than a master's degree, however. You couldn't play the politics.

"One thing bothers me, though. You're like Esau, in the Bible. You'd sell your birthright for a bowl of porridge. You live in the moment. This is what worries me. Say we were to give you money for college, then you get your degree and decide working's for the birds. You're going to live on a commune or be an artist or something. Never pay taxes. Then DVR wasted its money. The whole idea is to make you a *contributing* member of society. We're investing in you. We're saying, This young woman is going to be productive. She's going to have a place in society, not drop out of it. So I'm in a bind. We send you to college, we're taking a gamble."

Sell my birthright for a bowl of porridge? What did that mean? That I'd go for the easy thing? That I'd go for instant gratification, like an infant? And what did "live in the moment" mean? Was that like Be Here Now? I thought that was good. Maybe that was too Buddhist. Maybe Christians—and if I'd ever seen one, it was this guy—didn't think like that.

The creep wasn't going to send me to college.

"Here's my problem. I want to help you, but you only value what you work for. I want you to prove to me that you want this education. We'll pay for your tuition and books at community college; you couldn't get into a better school, with your high school record."

Why did relief always make me feel like crying?

"You'll still get your welfare. But you're going to

have to find your own transportation and day care for your child. I want you to feel you had to work for this opportunity."

Not the goddamn car and not the goddamn kid. Let the problem be anything but the car and the kid. If I had a car and a baby-sitter to begin with, I wouldn't be sitting in this old coot's office listening to how I'm an emotional and social basket case, based on ten hours of testing administered by a friggin' giant. Why didn't they just do the tarot cards? I was beginning to hyperventilate. How could he give me college in one breath and take it away in another? I couldn't talk. But I had to. I could feel my mouth contort, "Middlesex must be fifty miles away." The words came out in a shout, and I couldn't help it. "How am I supposed to get there?"

"I don't know. Maybe you can car pool it. Call the school. Find out who goes there from your area. Show some initiative. You have a lot of potential. Use it. You'll just have to figure it out. You're not going to get a free ride here."

CHAPTER 12

I'D been told by Mrs. Goldfarb I could get a college loan to buy a car. Now my mother split the blinds to take a first look at my new car in her driveway.

"Nice, huh?" I said.

"So clean," she said. "Better keep it that way."

That was the thing about my mother. I'd bought this beautiful fourteen-year-old with-a-rebuilt-engine emerald-green Volkswagen after four years without a car—which, incidentally, was not only going to take me to college but eventually off welfare—and all my mother had to say was, Better keep it clean? It's true, I'd been rude to my mother—probably, since puberty—but she had her faults too, and this took the cake. It was nearing last-straw time, and I don't mean just with her but my whole family.

I hadn't even bothered telling my father about college, since we hardly spoke and I knew my mother'd tell him anyway. Now tonight, after I'd arrived proudly with Jason in my new car, my father came home late for dinner, placed his walkie-talkie staticking next to his plate, and said, "So how many miles she got on her?"

"Ninety-seven thousand, but her engine's rebuilt."

"How much you say you paid for her?"

"Five hundred dollars."

He shook his head like there was a bee in it.

"Cupcake," Jason said.

"What?" my father said.

"That's what my mother named her."

My mother clicked her tongue.

"What?" I said. "She looks like she has white frosting." Her snout was painted white, which also made her look like a pit bull, but I preferred to see her as pastry.

"I don't know, Beverly," my mother said.

"You don't know what?"

"Never mind."

"You think it's childish to name a car. You think I'm crazy."

My father kind of snorted, but nobody answered.

"I think she looks like a cupcake," Jason said after a minute, which surprised me. Usually, even if we were having fun, even if it seemed like he was my best friend for one minute, as soon as we got in front of my mother, he turned traitor. He was forever threatening to tell my parents I smoked marijuana. Right now, he must've felt sorry for me.

"Me too," said Rose, who was now fifteen and smoking pot every morning, noon, and night of her life. At least there was one other person in my family I could halfway relate to.

I suppose the point wasn't so much the car but that everybody always had to make a big deal about what a weirdo I was, while they hardly noticed I'd be going to college, which to me felt like all those corny songs—"Climb Every Mountain," "The Impossible Dream." I mean, it felt like I'd moved heaven and earth, and then when I told my mother the good news, she'd said, "I thought you wanted a job. Now you got to go, what, four years?" Any normal parent would be proud that her kid was going to college, but not mine, mine was worried.

Then, when my brother walked in for the meatloaf dinner, it was the last straw. First of all, he was in uniform. And second of all, he stood next to me waiting for me to get up. My brother didn't live at home either, but he ate over as often as I did. When we showed up on the same night, I deferred the chair to him. But not this night.

"Bev, you're sitting in your brother's chair," my mother said.

"Who said it's his chair?"

"Move," my brother the blue bulk said.

I wanted to say, What're you going to do, asshole, clobber me with your billy club? but then who knew what would happen. He might pull me off the chair by my elbow. My father might yell. Whatever. I was too much of a coward to find out. I left the table, and as I seethed in the living room waiting for Jason to finish, I thought, How the hell did I get stuck with this family? A mother who seems afraid of her own flesh-and-blood daughter's being successful (because then I'd be different from her), growing up in a house where the men were served first and the women had to give their chairs to them. I swore my son would go to college and that never in his life would he think he deserved anything by virtue of his being born with a penis. Then I comforted myself with the thought that at least now I had my car and would be going to college. As soon as I heard the chairs scrape away from the table, I said, "Come on, Jase, we're going."

That was the spring of 1974, and I had to wait until the fall for my first day—when I woke up with the jitters. I stepped into the shower and combed my already pixie length hair with a straight-edged razor. As I watched the strands go down the drain, I thought how when I was little I'd made my mother set my hair with bobby pins for first days so I could look like my idol, Betty Boop, and make a good impression. I thought about how far I'd come. Now I walked by mirrors without looking, never wore makeup, shaved my legs, or plucked my eyebrows, and had even developed a vise-grip handshake. This was thanks to the women's consciousness-raising group I'd joined in New Haven soon after I got Cupcake.

By the time I stepped out of the shower, you could say I'd talked myself into feeling macho. I dried off, then put on my farmer's jeans and dropped a pen and a pencil in the pouch at my chest, which naturally made me think about writing something, which made me think about learning—which was the whole point of college, after all—and I got the jitters again. I figured now I'd have to prove I was as smart as I'd always thought. This would not be easy. I'd taken pride in being a borderline moron in high school and maybe now I'd pay for it. For all I knew, I might get thrown into remedial classes, in which case my pride would force me to jump out a window.

Down in the living room, I paused to look at Cupcake before making coffee. She shimmered like an emerald in the driveway. Behind her, a piece of paper skimmed along the gutter propelled by spurts of wind. I figured that paper was some kid's spelling homework. My chest filled, and I had to stop myself from crying. I could hardly believe my good fortune. I was joining the human race.

Then Jason came slouching through the room. He was capable of black Donofrio male moods, the silent broods. He could be the slug that came to breakfast, lunch, or dinner. And the last thing I needed right now was him acting like a dark cloud and reminding me of what had held me back from everything in life so far.

I knew he felt needy now because his mother was going off to college, but when he sat at the table and stared dazedly at nothing, I figured it was for attention and it pissed me off. It put me on the alert for kids-making-mothers-turn-cartwheels behavior. I said, "So what're you having for breakfast?"

"What is there?"

"What do I look like, the waitress? You want a menu?"

"Maybe I'll have Rice Krispies," he said.

"They're going to come floating to the table and pouring into your bowl, like a commercial?"

"No," he said, pushing his chair back hard and going to get the Rice Krispies.

"Today's my first day of college, remember?" I asked rhetorically, wanting to put the issue on the table.

"I know," he said, pouring milk on his cereal, then spooning two spoons of sugar in.

"Sugar's bad for you," I said.

"Can I come?" he said.

"No, you can't."

"Will you be home when I get home?" He was six years old and already knew how to act like an Italian husband.

"Aren't I always?"

"No."

"When have I ever left you home alone?"

"Once. I went over to Cassie's. Remember?"

"Oh, right. Excuse me. I was ten minutes late. You could've died."

"I could."

Being liberated did not just mean from men but from attitudes and kids, and Jason was not going to make me feel guilty about doing anything I wanted.

When he came back downstairs from brushing his teeth, I noticed his ears sticking out of his hair and that he was holding his Mighty Heroes lunch pail. For some reason the sight of him made me giddy. Then, when I hugged him goodbye and felt how small his bones were, how small he really was, I probably hugged him too long, because he squirmed and said, "Ma, the bus."

As I drove to school up winding roads, by cow pastures and cornfields, I slowed down for a blind curve and thought of Raymond's car accident. Where was Raymond, anyway? What did he do every day? Did he have new kids? Did he ever wonder about me? Then I wondered what the hell I was doing on my first day of college thinking about a junkie husband. Maybe good fortune made me think of bad. Maybe when things start to change, you want to hold on to something familiar.

Middlesex Community College was a bunch of flat, new, economically constructed buildings bunched up on a hill, with as much parking lot as class space. It was a school for commuters that was not long on beauty or aesthetics or little extras like protection from glaring sun in windows, but it was paradise to me. It was an inspiration of the sixties, a college of last resort. If you were a jerk-off in high school, this is where you could start over. If you were formerly too poor for college, you could go now, because Middlesex was cheap. Plus, they had counselors there to get you loans.

The education? Maybe because the students mostly had no money, we were often assigned one textbook per course that digested material for you instead of going to the sources, which was a little too much like high school for me.

Teachers? Well. There was Kirk Donnelly, my English Composition 101 professor, who had us bring in advertisements from magazines to show how pictures can do the job better than words; assigned us papers ("Describe a Room" . . . "Use a Paradox" . . . "Write a One-page Conversation"), which he collected and never handed back; and liked to talk for whole periods about his two-year career as a technical writer, producing manuals for the home repair of a brand of car I can't remember. On the other extreme was Phillip Henry, a Rhodes scholar who taught us philosophy by posing formerly unthought of questions, about the immateriality of the material world, the subjectivity of truth, and the circuity of time, which got me thinking so hard I felt brain cells growing.

Then there were my fellow students. There was one about my age, who, when asked to please read the essay assigned in English, picked up a blank piece of paper and pretended to be reading something she never wrote. I was sitting next to her when she did it, and seeing her actually pretend to read a blank page, for a good three minutes, threw me into a fit of laughing I couldn't stop. Mr. Donnelly smiled good-humoredly when she finished and said, "Maybe you'll share the joke, Bev?"

The woman shot me a dirty look.

I couldn't share the joke, because I didn't know myself what I found so paralyzingly funny. Except maybe it had brought to mind the ridiculous book reports I used to make up in high school. But making up book reports was nothing compared to this woman's performance, which was pure virtuosity. This was what you'd call unfulfilled potential. I admired her at the same time I thought she was a fool for not doing her assignments. Why come if you didn't want to work?

Maybe I was expecting everybody to have my experience, which was the same as gorging myself at a feast every day after living on nuts and raisins. I felt extremely lucky. I pitied the eighteen-year-olds in the back of the class, the gum-snapping, ˙hair-slouching, class-skipping, bad-habits-from-high-school students. They were probably being forced into attendance by their parents. But they were in the minority. In the front of the class, at the other end of the spectrum, were the highly polite grandmothers, some sharp-tongued middle-aged women, a nun, and a retired insurance salesman. The majority of the students, though, were about my age, which was twenty-four, and fellow victims of a previously rocky life. There were some GI-bill Vietnam vets, other mothers of small children, though they were mostly married, and then there were my two new friends—Arlene and Lizzy. Arlene was a native of Middletown and used to run with a girl's gang in high school. She had a scar on her shoulder from a knife fight and a tattoo on her knuckle. Now she wrote the most beautiful poems, using nature for metaphors, and worked as a bookkeeper. Lizzy had actually hitchhiked to California and back, sold her plasma to buy food, and lived in a tent by a river, then came home to find that her boyfriend, who supposedly played guitar like Jimi Hendrix, had offed himself the day before. Then Lizzy lost her voice and was committed to the state mental institution until the words came back four months later. Now she worked there with autistic children.

I met Lizzy and Arlene my second semester, after I'd already decided I had to get all A's. I had a lot to prove because of past life failure, but I also wanted A's because in my first month at Middlesex, I'd overheard a woman in my history class telling her neighbor that she was planning on getting a scholarship to Wesleyan University. I thought she was lying or at least deluded, because although Wesleyan was in the same town as Middlesex, it cost about a hundred times more and was mainly for kids with board scores of 1400 and diplomas from prep schools. I butted into her conversation just to see how far her lying would go. "How can you go to Wesleyan from here?" I asked her.

She said it was easy if you got all A's, because they had this scholarship called Etherington, for community-college students. I had an instantaneous fantasy. I'd get a scholarship. I'd be the only person in the whole school who was on welfare. A bunch of socialists with a severe case of societal guilt would befriend me and make me a working-class hero.

I went home and read the riot act to Jason. "I have to get all A's," I said, "and you have to help. If ever you see me reading a book or writing a paper, don't interrupt no matter what."

"What if I get cut?"

"Well, if you get cut."

"What if Andrew's throwing rocks?"

"Jason, use your own judgment."

"What if Annie's smoking butts?"

"Jason!"

"I don't like it when you study."

"You want me to stay poor and stupid and on welfare forever?"

"No."

"Then don't interrupt."

Silence.

"Okay?"

"I guess."

I developed a talent for pure concentration, which enabled me to hear absolutely nothing when I was reading or writing. In fact if Jason wanted my attention, he had to pull on my sleeve. When Jason had his friends up in his room on winter afternoons and they'd be arguing over who got to go first or accusing each other of cheating or playing hide-and-seek and making the ceiling sound like thunder above me, I'd be trying to figure the value of X, Y, or Z and hearing none of it. I succeeded in getting all A's—which wasn't hard once I figured all I had to do was tell the professor what he or she had already said; or if that was too much of a personal compromise, I simply had to make my own opinion as outrageous as possible. I applied to Wesleyan in the spring of 1975 but would not hear until the summer, because they needed my second-semester grades before they decided.

Finally it was summer, a Wednesday, and I'd gone to my last women's consciousness-raising-group meeting. We were breaking up because we were only five, and one woman was moving while another was leaving for the summer. We had a potluck dinner for the occasion and each of us brought a bottle of wine, which meant by the time we were finished eating, we were pretty loaded. Somebody put Joni Mitchell on the stereo, and one of the women got up and started dancing. Then we all got up. I had my eyes closed and was singing along, "I am on a lonely road and I am traveling traveling traveling, looking for something what can it be," and when I opened my eyes, I saw that my fellow women had taken their shirts off.

Now, the first thing I thought was, What would Fay say? With the exception of one, these women were homely; in high school I would've called them skanks and never given them the time of day. I pictured Fay's face at the window, laughing at me dancing with a bunch of half-naked skanks. Then I decided Fay and her reaction was her problem. I liked these women. They'd listened to my whole story—starting with a father who spied on me at the same time he ignored me, and ending with one feckless no-caring lay after another—and they'd listened with intelligence, good questions ("Why when you talk about making love do you always say *sex*? Do you make no distinction?"), and compassion.

Now I wanted to take my shirt off and join my friends. But it had been a long time since I went shirtless, since the age of eight to be exact, unless you wanted to count bouncing around in bed with a couple of dozen lovers, which I didn't.

I closed my eyes, took a breath, and lifted my shirt off. The air against my skin felt like the opposite of a caress. It was chilling. It was stimulating. To belabor a word, it was liberating. I realized it never would have felt so freeing if it hadn't been so long since I'd done it, and that there is something to be said for deprivation—which is the feeling you get when it's over.

The next morning, I got the envelope from Wesleyan. I'd been accepted. They were giving me an apartment on campus. My blood pressure dropped. Little sparkles swarmed over the page I was reading. I put my head between my knees to let the blood flow to my brain, and to let the information sink in. This meant I'd leave Wallingford, probably forever. I would leave one life and enter another. I lifted my head, and the sparkles were gone.

CHAPTER 13

SEVEN years after Raymond and I had moved into our mint-green duplex apartment as man and wife, my father, my mother, my brother, Jason, and I loaded two flowered living room chairs, given to me by the woman who'd made my wedding suit, Fay's mother's kitchen set, Jase's and my bedroom furniture, and boxes of everything else into my father's truck early on Labor Day morning 1975. I was to follow the truck in Cupcake. After everybody left, I went back into my house for a last look.

The house had a feeling of about-to-be, like it had already forgotten us and was waiting for its next experience. In my former bedroom, I riveted on some small black smears dotting the walls. They were the stains of dead mosquitoes from our first summer, before we had screens, when the mosquitoes made a feast of my pregnant body every evening, and then every morning as they slept, I whapped them to death with a rolled-up magazine. Looking at the remains of their massacre, which I never washed off, painted over, or hardly noticed for seven years, I wondered if that girl, who suffered through sleepless itchy nights rather than save herself with the purchase of screens, who could ignore her own dried blood on the walls for seven years, could ever be a normal person—and by that I meant could I survive, fit in, resist the urge to fuck up and ruin everything.

The house I'd been assigned on campus was not exactly beautiful. It was covered with haphazard gray shingles and had four small low-ceilinged rooms, with no light except for in the kitchen, plus brown-painted floorboards that slanted toward the middle. I decided to think of this place as my little college cottage. It had a porch and a grill made of rocks out back, bushes, flowers, and trees with squirrels jetting around the branches. It was on a pitted dead-end street at the edge of campus, called Knowles Avenue, and as we pulled up, I noticed a couple of kids riding their bikes down the hill next to the hockey rink across the street and wondered if they'd be friends of Jason's and who my friends would be.

It was still morning when we started unloading. My mother took command. "Your brother will help your father with the heavy stuff. I don't want you hurting your back. . . . Better put the bed there, away from the window or you'll get a draft. . . . If you put your canned foods closer to the stove, it'll be more efficient. . . . I always put the glasses above the sink. . . . What? Aren't you going to put paper on your shelves? . . ." She was out of hand. I was letting her get away with murder. What did she think, I was still that pregnant teenager she moved into the other apartment?

Everything had been moved in. My brother's friend had picked him up, and my father was walking around the hockey rink with Jason. My mother had cleaned the refrigerator, and was finishing the stove, when I sat on my bed, dropped my head into my hands, and thought how it was almost dusk and there might be a beautiful sunset, but how would I know? If

I'd moved in with friends, we might be sitting on the porch, ordering pizza, buying beers, having arguments about anchovies or no anchovies. Why'd I let my parents assume they'd do the moving?

This was my frame of mind when I stepped out of my bedroom and into the kitchen and spotted my mother moving the kitchen table to a different wall from the one I'd placed it against. "What the fuck do you think gives you the right to move that table?" I yelled.

"You'll get too much sun. I just thought . . ."

"You just thought you knew better. You just thought I was an imbecile. Get it straight. This is *my house*."

"Well." She puffed herself up.

I wasn't giving her a chance to talk. As far as I was concerned, she had no defense. "Ma, I know this is hard for you to take, but I'm different from you and I'm going to live a different life. Starting right here and now—with where I put the fucking Campbell's soup." I took a can and moved it from next to the stove to above the sink.

"Then I guess you don't need me anymore. We'd better go."

Now I felt like shit. "Well, we're moved in. You must be tired."

"Sonny," she called outside. She unclasped her cigarette case, took out a Kent, and lit it with a lighter. My father followed Jason in. He wiped his face with his handkerchief, crossed his ankles, and leaned against the stove. "All done?" he said.

"Come here," she said to Jason.

"You going already?" Jason said.

"You're going to miss your Mim, I know," she said.

Jason hugged her hips. She'd be a toll call away now. No way she'd stop by on her way to anywhere ever again. I felt like I was one of those Nazi death camp people shoving Jase into one line and her and my father into another.

She kissed Jase on the cheek, then pressed her pocketbook against her stomach and looked like she might cry as my father put his hand on the middle of her back and guided her out the door. "Don't be strangers now," she said through the car window as they pulled away.

The next morning at nine o'clock, Jase and I were standing in line at the Science Center, the modern building on campus, for registration. I'd been afraid people would stare at me because I'd be the only older person (twenty-five in a few days) and I'd be the only one with a kid. I was the oldest person there and the only one with a kid all right, but I was also the only one who noticed. Since I might as well be invisible, it was safe to take a look around, and what I saw were people cut from a different mold. The guys had over-developed heads and underdeveloped bodies and the girls had frizzy hair, backpacks, and frozen-faced expressions. I felt like the Student from Another Planet.

Jase had put on his *Night of the Living Dead* face and said, "How long do we have to stay here?"

"Until we get to the head of the line."

The line was the length of a football field. "Oh brother," he said, making like he might start crying. I was nervous enough, specifically, that once I got to the head of the line, they'd say, "Beverly Who? I'm sorry. You're not on the list."

"Jason! I don't need it," I said in a yell disguised as a whisper, then a tall lanky guy touched my shoulder and said, "Excuse me, is this the line for registration?"

"I guess," I said. What else would it be?

"Excuse me," he said, turning to the girl behind me. "Is this the line for registration?"

"Quite," she said.

Quite? Who in the world said *quite*? Was this what I'd have to choose from for friends? Why had I been in such a hurry to transfer from community college when I could've stayed there another year before I made this flying leap into whitebreadsville. A chubby guy butted in line in front of me. "Marcy!" he effused. "I can't believe you're going here too."

"Josh! My God. This is so cool," she said.

"I just got here," he said. "I can't tell you how much I miss my baby grand already."

Miss his *baby grand*? These kids were *rich*. Going to a school where a year's tuition could clothe, feed, and put a roof over a family of six's heads had been an expectation, like toilet paper in the bathroom, for most of these people. How could I ever relate? A drop of perspiration dripped from my temple. When the line moved forward, I stepped on the back of the fat kid's shoe.

He turned around.

"Excuse me," I said.

He smiled and turned back to Marcy.

"Ma, you did that on purpose," Jase whispered.

"So?"

"Why?"

"It makes me mad he's so rich."

"Why?"

"Because we're not, I guess."

"We're not poor, though?"

"No. And it's not even important to be rich. It's probably better to be poor. It's just that some people take it for granted and never think about people who aren't."

"I'm going to be rich," Jason said. "If I stepped on his shoe, you'd yell at me."

"What are you, my conscience?"

"What's that?"

"The voice inside your head that tells you when you're wrong."

"No."

"Just remember. You're the kid and I'm the mother."

"Yes, little girl," Jason said.

When I thought about this later, I wondered if I wasn't being as bad as my own mother by not allowing other people to be different—the way she wouldn't allow another place for the Campbell's soup.

Still, I was paralyzed by Fear of the Different and did nothing but study, which I expected would pay off. So when my professor asked me to come see him after I'd worked four days on, then handed in, my first English paper, I thought that maybe, like one of the professors at Middlesex had, he was going to invite me to contribute to the school magazine. Still, I was a bundle of nerves when I entered his office. Professors at Middlesex were regular people, while this professor had a goatee like a devil, an accent like Katharine Hepburn's, and did stuff like turn red in the face and burst forth lines by Wordsworth: "'Great God! I'd rather be a Pagan suckled on a creed outworn . . .'" This he said after storming into class and railing about a gas station attendant who'd just called him Bub. What if I used incorrect grammar? What if he asked me a question using a word I didn't know?

He sat in a leather chair across from me instead of behind his desk and smiled kindly. "You have trouble writing," he said.

I forgot to breathe. "I come from community college," I said by way of explanation.

"Yes," he said by way of saying he could tell.

Then he recommended I take a *remedial* writing course, for *no credit*. I could barely control my trembling lip in his office. I went into the bathroom and cried, sitting on the toilet. I could not flunk out, I simply couldn't. I knew I was the poor relation being let in through the back door of this place, but I'd thought—maybe academically, at least—I'd do all right. The humiliation was even more intense because I'd fantasized that when I graduated from college, I'd move to New York and be a writer. I took a handful of toilet paper and blew my nose. There was another roll of paper still wrapped up. That's Wesleyan for you, I thought as I walked out, extra paper in every stall. Not a speck of dirt or mess anywhere, every window in every ancient building opened with a lift of a finger, every lawn was manicured perfect, and there wasn't a dead branch on a single tree.

I'd only be depressed if I went home, so I wandered through the arts complex, which was a group of square limestone buildings scattered here and there under pine trees. The place was unreal. It looked like a moonscape. I passed a student reading a poem out loud under a tree. They were all over the place—skipping, singing, playing the flute. A woman stood under an arch and played the *bagpipes*. This, I thought, is a far cry from Susan Gerace playing "Taps" in the project.

Susan Gerace, who I'd heard had joined the marines, probably had no idea a place like Wesleyan existed. In Wallingford, if you crossed the street in the middle instead of on a corner, people would beep and you might get arrested. God forbid you should talk to yourself; they might lock you in an attic. One moonless night last week, I'd run as fast as I could with my arms outstretched across the athletic field, leaping across a puddle and splattering myself with mud, and

I'd thought one day I'd follow it up with skipping on a sidewalk. I never wanted to forget where I came from or what it was like there, because places like that were where most of the rest of the world lived—and as far as I could tell, they were populated by much more interesting people—but I didn't want to live there anymore, either.

I headed home finally, and thought of my neighborhood. The first week, the parents on my road had a meeting (three professors, their working wives, another single-mother student, and me) to organize communal day care. This meant I only had to be home one day a week at three o'clock, when our nine kids got out of school. Every other day, I was free until six. Jason had other parents to talk to and their houses to hang out in. He had friends who gave back rubs instead of boxing matches, painted rocks instead of throwing them, and were vegetarians instead of pickers of cigarette butts. They wrote a play and invited us parents. In it, the woman worked, came home exhausted, and then when her husband plopped a grilled-cheese sandwich in front of her for dinner, she said, "What about a vegetable?"

When I got home, I still didn't feel like going into the house and facing my books, so I decided to take a walk to the soccer field at the end of the road. I passed Jase and his friends on a porch rehearsing their new play, *The Martians Invade the White House*. Jason was playing the president. I heard him say, "What's a Martian?" and Brett say, "A Martian is what's in front of you," and I yelled, "Clever line."

"Hi, Ma," he said. "Where're you going?"

"Just for a walk."

"Oh," he said, which made me feel lonely, because he didn't ask if he could come, and envious, because he'd fit right in and I hadn't.

Once on the soccer field, I looked to my right at the school for juvenile delinquents up on the hill. I was looking for a pregnant girl I'd seen pumping on the swing set, but she wasn't there. I wondered, like I had so many times since the first day I'd seen her, if this obsession I had with seeing her wasn't a little unhealthy. Was I hanging on to the past? But her being at a neighboring school and our having so much in common was too much of a coincidence to ignore. Besides, maybe I could help her somehow. Maybe one day I'd get up the courage to talk to her. She had appeared in my dreams once already. She'd been on the hill pumping and pumping, but she was older and she wasn't pregnant. I wondered if she was me.

I went home finally, opened my *Norton's Anthology,* and forced myself to read.

By the spring, things were different. For one thing, Bub, the professor, had given me an A−, and I'd learned some valuable lessons in my remedial-writing course, such as using connectives like *therefore* and *consequently* in my papers, and never ending them with a firm conclusion, because conclusions were too facile, not to mention fragile. And for another, I hadn't seen the pregnant girl for some time, and had almost forgotten about her, when I spotted a kid tear-assing down the hill and through the field, escaping. I felt exhilarated. It was all I could do to keep myself from shouting, "Go, man, go." I prayed he made it. I prayed the pregnant girl did too. Then, a few days later, Cupcake was stolen. I cursed my rotten luck. I admonished myself for being so cavalier about her, for never locking her and leaving the keys on the floor.

My father put an all-points out on Cupcake, and miraculously, a week later, he got a call from a cop in Bridgeport, seventy miles away, who said he'd recovered Cupcake from a ghetto called Hell's Gate. A key obviously made in metal shop was in her ignition, though her own keys were still on the floor. Then, a couple of weeks later, exactly the same thing happened. Cupcake was stolen, found in Bridgeport, and returned.

I made up a story. Then I believed it. The girl had left the school after she'd had her baby and had been forced by her mean parents to give it up for adoption. But her boyfriend was still locked up. He'd seen Cupcake somehow and had made a key to fit her. Then, when he got his chance, he climbed through the boiler-room window, ran down the hill and across the field, and stole her, driving all the way to Bridgeport, where the girl lived. He got caught, but undaunted, he did the same thing again. This time, Cupcake had been retrieved, but the kid hadn't been caught. He was with the girl, who thought this was the best thing that had happened to her in her life when really it was the worst. In fact, she was probably getting knocked up again that very moment.

I wondered if just as it was Cupcake's destiny to be a vehicle of escape it was mine to be linked with pregnancy and prematurely ended childhoods that last forever because they never were complete. It might be true and it might not. Only time would tell, but meanwhile, I had proof things could change. I'd made friends with people who were different. The first was Sally Dummerston, who became my best friend. She had two daughters and was the other single mother on the block. When I'd met her my first week at school, she'd introduced herself by saying, "Hi. I'm a Woman in Transition, too." Women in Transition was a category the university lumped us dozen or so single mothers into, and at the time I'd thought, anybody who introduces herself as a category is not a person I'm interested in saying two words to. Besides, she had cheerleader written all over her. But then Jason and Sally's oldest daughter, Elizabeth, were best friends and circumstances kept bringing us together, until one night we got drunk and I turned Sally on to pot for the first time in her life and she confessed that she wasn't only a Woman in Transition but a Daughter of the American Revolution and then we giggled for a good ten minutes.

Sally and I made a family with our kids. We cooked dinners together and ate mostly at Sally's, because she had a dining room with a piano on which she played Chopin, a candelabra, and cloth napkins. I learned about WASPs from Sally. I said to her, "But what do you *want?*" and she said, "It doesn't matter," or, "Whatever you like," when whatever it was did matter. Finally, I caught on that I was supposed to ask her four or five times before I could expect the truth, because before that, Sally figured that to tell the truth was impolite. She smiled and was polite to everybody, even the troupes of boring, ugly, single professors who dropped by morning, noon, and night unannounced to get flashed by Sally's smile and soothed by her graciousness. I know for a fact she loathed some of these guys for being smug or pompous or dull, but she offered them wine or beer and put Linda Ronstadt on the stereo and pretended to listen to them anyway. When our kids were acting like idiots, she said, "Now, children," while I said, "Shut up."

When Sally graduated a year before me, Jase and I were sad, but there were compensations: We weren't really losing them because they were only moving to New Haven, and I had asked the university for and had been granted her house, which was much larger and nicer than mine, then I'd invited two men ex-students to join me as roommates.

Their names were both James and they were big and gentle, like golden retrievers. I'd met them in a class called "Toward a Socialist America" and they'd stayed on after their graduation to found a political magazine. They were the type of guys who handed out leaflets and jumped all over the university about this injustice or that discrimination. They'd get drunk with their friends and stay up until dawn debating social democracy versus socialism, throwing words like *hegemony* around and ending by actually singing "We Shall Overcome" at sunrise. They had hundreds of friends who visited our house. Two or three stayed for a couple of months. We had huge dinners and grand dancing parties that spilled onto the street. We sang in the car on trips to the store or laundromat with Jason. We played cowboy family during dinners. Sometimes we read poems by candlelight while we ate dessert; other times we pushed the dining table into a corner, and Jase and I taught them *Saturday Night Fever* dances we'd memorized from seeing the movie five times over.

Like Fay's moving in with me back in 1971, this was a dream come true. There were two guys living in my house, shooting baskets with Jason and reading him stories, which was as good as any father; plus, these guys didn't lionize me, exactly, for being working-class, but they were uncomfortable with their own social advantages and awfully curious about me and my family. "Does your mother vote like your father automatically, or does she make up her own mind? Is her factory unionized? What does your father think of your living with two guys?"

CHAPTER 14

THEY got the answer to that question soon enough. My father came by to hang a spice rack that I'd requested he make me for my birthday, and didn't offer his hand for shaking when I introduced him. Naturally, this pissed me off.

The next Sunday, I showed up at his house wearing a see-through blouse, then struck up a conversation with my mother. "You ever been to a porn shop, Ma?" I said.

"No," she said, glancing nervously at my father, who was pretending not to listen as he watched the Giants game on TV.

"They have this doll. You blow it up human size. It's got a hole . . ."

My father left the room, then slammed into the cellar, where in a moment we heard the screech and drone of his electric saw. This was the first time in memory my father had ever abandoned a Giants game. I considered it a victory.

"Good," I said to my mother. "Want to watch the Bette Davis movie on channel five?"

"Shame on you," she said.

College had not made me your model daughter. Maybe I was worse than ever. I purposely used words they didn't understand, because I refused to curtail my speech to bow to ignorance, and insisted on criticizing my parents' way of life to my mother. "How can you stand to have that television on nonstop? It's like mental Novocain."

"You know your father."

"And you have nothing to say about anything that goes on in your own house?"

"Please, Beverly, don't start."

At Thanksgiving, I suggested my father and brother do the dishes. I got laughed at. I turned on my mother. "You put up with it. What's the matter with you? You must like it. You're a martyr."

"You do what you want in your house and I'll do what I want in mine," she finally said, and I shut up about it.

But that didn't mean my mother shut up about me. One weekend my last semester at college, I dropped Jason off, as I often did on Friday nights, leaving him there until Sunday. This Friday, she said, "Honest to God, Beverly. Don't you ever look at your son? Look at him. Just look at him."

"What? What?" Jase said, looking down at himself.

The kid had dirt under his nails, greasy hair lying like strings on his forehead, and rumpled, obviously worn-too-many-times clothing. Until she'd mentioned it, I hadn't even noticed. I thought back and could not tell you the last time he'd bathed. I felt terrible about this, and on the drive home from my mother's house, it set me thinking. First I thought about Sasha, the woman who lived upstairs from me for a year and a half in the gray shingled house. She had a three-year-old son named Armond, who, if you asked me, she was overprotective of. For this reason she never joined in on our communal day care. Armond hardly left the apartment, even to play in the yard. Periodically, Sasha would go off her rocker and stomp down the stairs with Armond under her arm like a football and knock on my door. When I answered it, her face contorted with anger, she'd say, "I'm taking Armond to the orphanage. He's a very bad boy. I can't stand him anymore." Then Armond would cry and Sasha would make him promise to be good, then end the dramatics. Or if she was really furious, she carried it further, dragging the kid to the car then off to some building she told him was an orphanage. Anyway, one day I'd gone somewhere and not returned until dusk. Maybe Jason had done something to piss her off, like tease Armond, or maybe Sasha was just being a nut, I don't know, but when I came home she was standing in the hallway livid. "You're a terrible mother," she said. "You don't deserve to have a child. How could you leave an eight-year-old for five hours? Five hours unattended?" At the time I thought to say, At least I don't threaten my kid with an orphanage, but instead I just shrugged.

Now I thought of what Sasha had said in light of my mother's pointing out the physical neglect of Jason, and I thought the two of them had something. I was becoming a more terrible mother than ever. I wondered, in fact, if I weren't dissipating altogether.

There was plenty of evidence. For one thing, I was smoking marijuana before class more and more frequently. For another, I had on occasion taken to mixing Kahlúa with milk and substituting it for coffee in the morning. And last semester I'd gone to my dean, sat Jason on my lap as evidence, then asked to drop a class. I said, "It's unfair that at this university there are students who have a maid come in to clean their bathroom when I have to carry the same course load, cook and clean for a kid, plus work part-time at a job (as an editorial assistant, ten hours a week)." The dean had simply agreed and said, "Sure. If you want, drop the class. We understand it's more difficult for you single mothers."

That gave me more time, so what I did was take up with a drug dealer named Sonny Tune, who drove a Lincoln Continental and carried a gun in a briefcase. Half the reason I went with the guy was to be able to tell people and to see the look on the Jameses' faces when I let it drop that Sonny kept his gun under the bed every time he slept over. Sonny didn't last long though. Since he could only call me from phone booths and I could only reach him at the same, he was hard enough to get in touch with, but once a judge put a subpoena out on him, it was impossible.

Next, this final semester, a couple of weeks before, in fact, I went to a bar in Hartford and picked up this muscle-bound ape named Rocky who drove a white Caddy. When we went into his car to snort some cocaine, he rolled up a thousand-dollar bill for the purpose and said, "Do you swing?"

"What do you mean?" I said.

"You know. You and me and my buddy Sal?"

"Sure," I said, "we'll arrange it." Then gave him a fake phone number.

So this day in the car, envisioning the way Jason had looked when I dropped him at my mother's, I thought he resembled a nine-and-a-half-year-old David Copperfield after his mother died, and I decided I should stop this slip-sliding before I got carried away. I figured my dissent was the result of the minor breakdown I might be having due to my imminent graduation from Wesleyan.

Wesleyan had given me an excellent education and paid for it, besides being like a finishing school preparing me for the upper middle class. It had given me a house and shoveled my walks. It had been like the ideal father to me, but in the end it would be just like my father of flesh and blood, who'd said so long ago, "Once you leave, you're not coming back."

Let's face it, I hadn't done such a good job on my own the first time around. I figured it was no coincidence I was using men as a means to disintegrate given what success I'd had using them for the same purpose in the past—conscious or unconscious—starting with Skylar Barrister in the backseat of a car parked by a garbage dump.

I decided to watch out and begin a campaign of good health and better morals. I would begin by instituting bath time every night and by making a date for the movies the next weekend with Jason.

As it happened, the week between my resolve and our date, Cupcake broke down. The mechanic said she needed a new alternator, which would have to wait because I had no money to fix her. Seeing Cupcake covered by a mound of snow in the backyard felt like an omen. It was my last semester. I was about to graduate, and maybe I would leave better off, with a college diploma, but I might also be reduced to the status of carless person. What would that mean?

I was studying a lot of literature and seeing symbolic meanings and foreshadowings in everything. I was being silly. I cheered myself up. There were plenty of students who went four years to college without ever having a car. I could walk to all my classes. I could shop at the little, though more expensive, corner market. I could hitch rides with neighbors. Eventually, I'd save the money to fix her. It would work out.

On Saturday evening, the night of our date, it was freezing out. It had snowed for eight hours and there were mountains of snow bordering all the roads and driveways. Ice covered the paths. Jase and I bundled up and made off to see *Dog Day Afternoon* at the theater on campus, stopping first to buy Jason some penny candy at the corner market.

As soon as we felt the blast of heat in the lobby, Jason took off his mittens and stuck his hand in his pocket to fondle his candy and found there was nothing left but a single, miniature peanut butter cup. "Oh no!" he said. "They fell out the hole." His festive aspect collapsed before my eyes. Immediately, I felt guilty for the hole in his pocket, both because it was there and because I hadn't known it. We sat down. Jason, who'd been chatting lightheartedly with me on our walk, was transformed into a black hole in the seat next to me. I didn't sense him lightening up until midway through the movie, when he laughed at Al Pacino's transvestite girlfriend/boyfriend. Then, as we were exiting the theater, we ran into an acquaintance named Dan who Jason knew to have a car. Jason whispered to me, "Do you think Dan can give us a ride?"

This reminder that once again in my life I was stuck without a car, as well as his suggestion that I rely on a *man* to help us out, irritated me no end. "We're walking," I hissed under my breath. "It's good for you."

Once outside, Jason started chattering his teeth and taking tiny steps like a Chinaman to signify how cold he was. Almost beside myself with loathing by now, I grabbed his shoulder and turned him around to pull his hood up. "Ouch!" he yelled, surprising me.

People stopped and looked at us.

I dropped to my knees in front of him, said, "Hold still," and yanked his hood string so hard it broke in my hand.

"You broke it!" he screamed, which surprised me

again. Next, he yelled, "You're *nuts*! I'm running away." Hysterics were not part of Jason's repertoire. Whining, moping, arguing, yes, but hysterics definitely not. While I stood there kind of dumbfounded, he took off, leaving me in the snow, with half of the school staring, like I was a child beater.

I watched this little black figure gliding along the snow until it disappeared behind a mound and all I could see was his black sailor's cap above it, which turned around every now and then to see if I followed. My chest felt fluttery, like I was on the verge of laughing. But Jason was getting farther and farther away, so I began running. When I was close enough, I alternately ran and walked to keep him no more distant than a hundred yards. With my kid running away from me like I was his enemy, an instance of recent child abuse came to mind. He'd had a friend over from school and they were firing rubber-tipped arrows at me and the Jameses as we prepared a complicated Mexican dinner for one of our socialist professor friends. Jason must've been using us for target practice for about half an hour when my ability to concentrate on what I was doing and ignore kid disturbance reached its threshold and it dawned on me that I did not have to take this. In fact this was ridiculous to allow. So I said to one of the Jameses, "Grab that Indian." He did, and I took an egg and cracked it on Jason's head.

I thought it was a riot. Jason did not get the humor. He was outraged. His face turned red and his eyes bulged from his head and he said, "You're *crazy*!" then he ran upstairs and locked himself in the bathroom. He would not let me in, but eventually he did let the Jameses in. Later, they told me that Jason had cried and said that he was going to become a lawyer and specialize in the rights of children, which I'd heard before.

He also said that now he was afraid his friend would go back and tell his class that his mother had cracked an egg on his head. Which had never occurred to me. Now, as I saw Jason stop at the crossroads—where if he took a left he'd really be running away, but if he took a right he'd be nearly home—I stopped too, thinking that I may have been cursed by being saddled with a kid so young, but that Jason had been just as cursed by being saddled with me. He took a right. My heart stopped pounding in my ears and I walked the rest of the way. I took my time in the house, too. I could see the little puddles left by his boots on his way to the stairs to his room. I put some cider on the stove and smoked a cigarette while waiting for it to warm. I knew we had to talk, but I didn't know what I would say. I looked at the guitar he'd pretended to play earlier in the evening, standing on the hassock and bouncing on his knees. Sometimes when Jason lightened up, we could have a good time. Sometimes he could be a regular ham. We could sing in the kitchen for hours and disco dance like crazy.

He was lying in bed, the covers over his head. I sat next to him. "You're an asshole," I said to make a joke.

"Is that why you chased me all the way home?" he said. "To call me an *asshole*?" He was crying now.

Suddenly, I was mad again. "You made me feel guilty, about not having Cupcake."

"What?"

"You know she's broken and I don't have the money to fix her, yet you had to complain and complain. It's not my fault."

"That's not what it was," he said. "I wanted a ride because I was cold and tired. That's not what it was." Now he was sobbing and choking from not catching his breath. I lifted him onto my lap and rocked him. I'd thought Jason was trying to make me feel guilty when he'd simply been tired. He hadn't been thinking of me at all. Just as I hadn't been thinking of him.

Did I always believe that everything Jason said and did was for the purpose of eliciting some effect in me? Was I that egocentric? Was this a result of my thinking his being born had ruined my life, so I forgot the kid had a life of his own and only thought about how his life affected mine? Had my personality been so un-formed when I had him that he simply became a part of it, like a birch grafted onto an elm?

I stroked his back. His face was hot and wet against mine. I hoped that his grandmother's thinking the sun rose and set in him would overcome his having been invisible to me.

In a month or so I got the car fixed, and in May of that year, 1978, I graduated with a bachelor of arts de-gree in English. In June, I began looking for an apart-ment in Little Italy—it was cheap and safe—in New York City, where I was determined to make my life and my fortune, whatever that would be. I found my apartment on June 24, on the same evening I totaled Cupcake.

I was alone and exiting Central Park when I didn't see the meridian separating the incoming from the out-going traffic and sailed right over it, landing splat in the middle of the "in" side. The engine shut off and her lights went black. When I stepped out, I saw that her tires had flattened out to her sides and her belly was flush against the asphalt. I flagged down a Checker cab, which crunched into her rear end as it pushed her against the curb on Fifth Avenue, where I left her. When I returned the next morning for a visit, her doors were flung open, her battery gone, the contents of her glove compartment strewn all over, and the golf ball that had been her gear-shift handle ripped off and gone forever. I sat by her on the bench all day and wept.

I'd planned on giving Cupcake away anyway. She was eighteen years old, not worth much money, and I'd been told I wouldn't need her in New York. She'd be too difficult to park and expensive to keep. Now I wished I'd never driven her to New York at all, that I'd parked her in my parents' backyard, where she'd have been safe, drilled a hole in her roof, and planted a tree through it.

PART
TWO

CHAPTER 15

WHEN we reach my par-
ents', it's nine in the evening, pitch-black out, and no
longer pouring rain. We see my mother at the window
and in a second she's at the door. She doesn't wait until
we've stepped out of the car before she starts talking,
"So you finally made it. What weather."

"I bet she's been waiting at the window for three
hours," Jason whispers to me.

"Only rain," I say.

"But in all that traffic?"

Jason lopes up the hill to the front door, where my
father is now standing behind my mother. My mother
kisses Jason while my father shakes his hand and puts
his other hand on my son's shoulder, which is taller
than his. "The college kid," he says, giving Jase a pat.
This trinity in the doorway, a lawn length away,
makes me feel strange. Lonely or melancholy, aware,
at least, of how nothing stays the same.

We go into the house, and I feel like a clairvoyant. I
can predict exactly what will happen in the next half
hour. My mother will ask a million questions about
the journey, as though we'd come halfway across the
world through continents deluged by monsoons when
all we did was drive two and a half hours north on the
interstate from Manhattan in the rain. Jason will cut

himself a piece of whatever she's baked for the occasion, eat it, then go up to the attic recreation room, otherwise known as his room. The Castro convertible will already be made into a bed. He'll take his science-fiction book out of his backpack, lie on the bed with the remote for the cable next to him, and settle in for the night. Since he became a teenager, when he comes to his grandparents', he seeks solitude in corners like a cat. At home in New York, because our apartment is so small, he either shuts the door to his room or goes down to the Polish bar a couple of blocks away, where he plays chess with an old Romanian who wears paper bags for hats, or he plays pool for hours and hours, for as long as he holds the table.

Is this sad?

My kid had no cozy living room with family portraits on the wall, no clan of siblings fighting for space on the couch. No. My son had only me. More to the point of my feelings right now, I had only my son and a cat named Lou to keep me company in my apartment. And now, with his imminent departure to the upstairs room, I am anticipating the grander, deeper, more permanent departure to college that will come the next day. But what's the big deal? Why the moroseness? Hadn't I been shaking my fist at the ceiling, wishing for solitude and an apartment of my own? Hadn't I been chomping at the bit for the day I'd be minus one guilt-inducing kid to take care of? Then, like a flash of lightning, I'm struck with an image of not so long ago. Of his waiting for me to get out of a car so he could walk with me hand in hand. I'm being dramatic. I can't help it. Endings do that to me. Besides, it's in my blood.

Everything goes as predicted, and once Jason has gone off to his room, my father shifts focus back to the

TV and my mother and I sit in the kitchen with cups of tea in front of us. My mother stirs some milk in and says, "My prayers were answered."

"Ma," I say. "Do you actually pray?"

"Of course. What do you think I am? Of course," she says, offended.

"Well, you know, some people use it as a saying. I was just wondering if you really pray or use it as a saying."

"Every night. I prayed for Jason to get all A's and get a scholarship. Then, when he did, I said I'd say so many extra Our Fathers and I forget how many Hail Marys. I pray that you'll do good with your writing. I don't ask for anything for myself. Just give me the strength."

I'm a little shocked by this revelation. I mean, I knew my mother believed in God, if only by the amount of times she'd say, "See? God punished you," when, for example, I'd dropped a gallon of milk on my toe. And her most common curse evoked the Holy Family: "Jesus, Mary, and Joseph, if you kids don't shut up, I'll kill you." But she never went to church, except for baptisms and funerals. She said the priests were mostly Irish and money hungry. But now that I think of it, there's always been that string of mother-of-pearl rosaries hanging on her bedpost, which I'd assumed was for decoration, like the crucifix above her bed.

Now I have the vision of my mother, this short lady (my mother has shrunk about two inches since my childhood) with a big nose and hair that's more pink than brown because the gray refuses to take the dye anymore, lying on her back, clutching her rosary beads to her flat chest, praying for me and Jason and the rest of her family night after night for years and years and years. I figure I'm lucky. How many people have a mother praying for them every night? But knowing my mother, she was probably praying for the wrong thing—like the time I told her I'd be going to college and she said, "I thought you wanted a job." But then, I've been thinking lately that maybe there's a big design, that the end is already there in the beginning and there's nothing we can do about it, not in a lifetime. Nothing we can do about the events, but plenty we can do with them. It all comes down to the way we look at things.

Right now, I'm thinking my mother's looking at me like I'm a heathen. She says, "I bet you don't even remember your prayers."

"I remember," I say.

Now Jason walks through the kitchen on his way to brush his teeth but is bushwhacked by my mother, who has come back down to earth for her role as mother-provider. "I bought you soap, you know, a big pack—economy—shampoo, toothpaste, Q-tips, shaving cream, a couple of notebooks, pens, socks, underwear; can you think of anything else?"

"No," Jason says.

"No," I say.

"You got sheets, towels, a pillow?"

"Yes," Jason says.

"Yes," I say.

"You got a raincoat, boots?"

"No," Jason says, when I was about to say yes. "I don't wear a raincoat or boots," he says. That's the difference between Jason and me. I'll lie 100 percent of the time to get my mother off my back, Jason only 50. Now he's got her going.

"What? You'll catch your death. What're you going to do when it rains?"

"Drown," Jason says, and I laugh.

"And you," my mother says. "I suppose you never make him."

I just shrug. It's the old debate. Good mother, bad mother. Is it worse to have an overprotective one who tries to keep you a kid forever or one who verges on neglecting you and therefore makes you responsible for yourself? Did I neglect Jason out of indifference? I don't think so. It was just our habit. We'd started out as one kid looking after another, and things haven't changed too much, even though I'm now about to turn thirty-six. I went to the source and asked Jason once. We were at a diner in our neighborhood in downtown New York. I was buttering a piece of bread and Jason was sinking an ice cube in his Coke with a straw. He was being moody and uncommunicative, a common state since he had started to sprout pimples a year before. He was fifteen at the time.

"Do you wish you had a real mother?" I said.

He smiled. "We're more like roommates than mother and son, aren't we?"

"Yeah," I said, startled to hear coming out of his mouth what I'd often thought to myself. "But do you ever wish we were more normal?"

"No," he said. "It's better we're this way."

He might've just been trying to shut me up, so I continued with the questions—in search of the truth or, maybe, reassurance. "If I were a regular mother"—I helped him along—"I wouldn't let you play pool at Stella's."

"Right."

"Or stay home from school when you felt like it."

"And you'd probably make me make my bed every day."

"But I'd also cook you breakfast and dinner."

"That's true," he said.

Jason and I grocery shopped together, and he cooked as often as I did, although his repertoire was limited to tacos and hamburgers and frozen dinners (for himself, not for me), while I could be a good cook when I felt like it. Half our meals were eaten at the very diner we were sitting at—an entree of meat, mashed potatoes, and a vegetable for $2.95. Or we ate take-out from the Chinese restaurant around the corner or Pete's A Pizza on 14th Street.

"Still," I said. "You're glad?"

"Ma, you're a good mother," he said.

He might've just said it to spare my feelings, but that was as good as his telling the truth. Jason, I was aware, had become my friend. It started when we moved to New York. Neither of us knew another soul but each other, and for the first time in my life, I couldn't dump Jason on my mother and his loyalty shifted from her to me. Maybe it began when we heard gunshots in the night and talked through the wall dividing our rooms in the darkness. "Did you hear that, Ma?"

"Yeah."

We walked all over the city, going to double-feature movies, shopping in thrift shops, staring at people on the street. We held hands everywhere we went. When I was with Jason, the men with menacing eyes and animal noises coming from their mouths left me alone out of respect for the young man, or maybe respect for motherhood.

When I discovered a great bar a couple of blocks west, with pictures of Al Pacino and Frank Sinatra on the wall, I went there for beers with Jason, who the owner treated to Cokes and chips. Jason learned to play pool and, on Friday nights, at the age of ten, could sometimes hold the table for as long as two hours. But after seven or eight months of camaraderie, I met Nigel. Nigel was eleven years older than I and a painter. He'd been to parties with John and Yoko and lived in the Chelsea Hotel, where Sid murdered Nancy. I was impressed. He carried a camera everywhere and documented my every sigh, dirty look, and burst of laughter with the click of his camera. I made up to cosmetic companies for all those years I had never used their products, because I'd become a twenty-eight-year-old walking, talking, club-hopping Barbie.

Jason hated Nigel. Probably because he was a nut. And looked like it. He had blond hair that stood on end and intense bulging blue eyes that never softened. He was afflicted with severe separation anxiety, which meant he couldn't let me out of his sight. At the time this was fine with me, because it meant he'd support me if I quit my job as a secretary, which I'd taken to feed me and Jason while I continued doggedly writing my short poems, if you can call them that: "I purple my hair my eyes my mouth. My cheeks I paint blue. I make myself into a bruise for you." And I kept a notebook of graffiti for future reference: "Lick me, eat me, make me write bad checks. Lexington Avenue Line, Canal Street, 1979." Maybe I liked that line so much because Nigel could've written it. The guy was a raging alcoholic who threw money around like toilet paper. So once the money ran out from a painting he'd sold, we had to leave the beautiful cathedrallike loft he'd sublet and I got a job typing on a computer three nights a week.

Meanwhile, poor Jase was being ostracized in an all-Chinese school, where he excelled in his schoolwork but had no social life whatsoever, except when he stopped at the post office on his way to school to buy some first-issue stamps that he'd sell to the kids for a profit. Soon, though, after we lost the sublet, we moved to an empty two-hundred-year-old building that was no more than an abandoned construction site. We were planning on renovating it, but in the meantime we slept next to cement bags and walked up stairs made of cinderblocks and washed dishes with a hose poised over a floor drain. Jason met two boys in our new neighborhood, Juno and Amos, kids of sculptor parents who'd lived in a camper on the streets for a couple of months, and for a year in a ditch in New Mexico, so Jase had something in common with his new friends. They began shining shoes in bars for spending money, while I began to seriously dissolute in the same bars with Nigel, making my fear about using men to slip-slide away a reality. Finally, at the bar around the corner, there appeared a gypsy fortune-teller who for five dollars threw three pyramid-shaped dice and told me to ditch Nigel. "And who is the boy?" she said. "The one with light hair and light eyes? He is crying for you. Alone. The man will eat you alive. Leave him, and go with the boy. That is your salvation."

I took her advice and Jason, and I dumped Nigel, who wasn't what you'd call easy to get rid of, because after we moved to our current apartment, a fifth-floor walk-up perched on a corner of Avenue A in the East Village, Nigel called every other minute, then began to appear after midnight, on the corner, calling to my window, "Beverly, Beverly, I love you, you asshole."

Eventually, like a bad dream, he went away, and I decided I had to get back on track. I would enroll one day in graduate school for writing, but right then, typing three nights a week barely paid the rent, so I added nude modeling to my résumé. Which I thought would be good therapy, considering my inhibitions about being nude in front of people unless I'm having sex.

Jason was twelve and disapproved. One night we were walking to the movies and out of the blue he comes up with, "What's a call girl?"

"A high-class whore you make a date with on the phone."

"That's what you are."

"What?"

"Men call you on the phone and ask you to take your clothes off, don't they?"

With the onset of Jason's puberty, it was beginning to feel like Jason was trying to step into the role of my father. He always wanted to know where I was going, what time I'd be home, and then how much money I'd spent. He told me he was planning on becoming a millionaire and then he'd give me an allowance, but no more than a thousand dollars a month, because I'd just squander it.

I'd maintained since the sixties that sex was healthy and good and should not be hidden from children, but I was beginning to think twice. Especially after I left my diaphragm out to dry and Jason said, "Ma. Tell me the truth. Don't you think it's disgusting to leave that thing out, in the kitchen?" We had no bathroom, only a toilet in a closet. The tub was in the kitchen, as well as our one and only sink, so where else to put a diaphragm to dry after washing but on the shelf above the sink? But that was the last time I did that. I began to sleep with men only on weekends, when Jason went to my parents', which he did all the time, taking the two-hour train ride to New Haven, where he was picked up by my father and mother.

Then one year, Jason was almost fifteen, and he

came home from six weeks at camp six inches taller. "I can't believe it," Jase said. "Everything looks so small. I'm taller than you. I bet I can lift you up." Then he did.

The tables were turned. The balance was tipped. He was taller than me. He became the kid and I the parent.

Jason made friends with a twenty-one-year-old carpenter and began hanging out at the Polish bar down the avenue playing pool. I had quit nude modeling, was enrolled in graduate school, and spent most of my time at home writing and reading whenever I wasn't at work. I stopped having sex; Jason started having girlfriends. A whole succession of them. Then one night, when he was a junior in high school, I came home from dinner with a friend and spotted a girl's green leather jacket on a chair in the living room. The door to Jason's room was closed. I went to sleep, and in the morning the jacket was still there. I went out to buy the paper and have a cappuccino. When I came back, the jacket was gone and Jase's door was open. He was reading on his bed. "Who was here last night?" I asked him.

"Carol," he said. "She's cool. She goes to Bard and pays for school by making porn movies. But she's not really the type. You know what I mean?"

Christ, I thought to myself, is my kid going to be fascinated with wild girls because his mother was one? This Carol was the second girl who'd slept over and about the fifth girl Jase had gone out with. Was he heading for a fiasco love life like I had? Would he use women to make a demolition derby of his life, like mine? I figured we were past due for a talk.

"When I was young," I began, feeling like an idiot, uncomfortable with my new role, like I was in a situation comedy or something, "I romanticized creepy people. I was attracted to the seamy side of life. I was very impatient to have experiences. But you know, Jase, you're only innocent once, and when you lose it, it's gone. Gone forever. So don't be in such a hurry, okay?"

"I'm not like you," he said.

I didn't have to reflect much on that one. The kid and I were like night and day, starting with our appearance. I was as dark as he was light. Plus, Jase was a loner. He liked to have one friend and not a group like I had. He got all A's, worked in a bookstore, and never asked me for money.

"Sex should be about love." I changed the subject in order to get to it.

"I know."

"So how can you sleep with all those girls?"

"Who said I had sex with them?"

"Didn't you?"

"Ma, why are you so obsessed with this?"

Was I being obsessed? Did I have a sexual fixation? Was I a maniac about it where my son was concerned, like my father had been with me? This definitely could be a case of generational repeating. This was not the first such conversation I'd had with Jason. I'd told him to always carry rubbers and not to leave it up to the girl to use birth control, because girls had mysterious, unconscious wishes for pregnancy and cannot be trusted. I told him liberated men always shared responsibility. Speaking of which, this would be a good time to put another word in. "I hope you're using birth control."

"Let's drop it, okay?"

"What if you got a girl pregnant? That would be just wonderful."

"I wouldn't mind having a baby."

"*What*? Are you trying to make me crazy? I thought you were going to college."

"I could go to college with a kid. You did."

I felt like grabbing my hair with both hands and pulling, but I got a grip on myself. This called for a modulated voice and sensible words, because obviously, Jason was trying to incite a one-woman riot. "Do you know about the urge to repeat?" I said very slowly and calmly. "People repeat things for generations and generations without being aware. I got pregnant. Mim got pregnant. Grammy got pregnant. Three generations. Don't make it four."

"Grammy was pregnant? Who told you?"

"Mim. A long time ago. Didn't I tell you?"

"I don't remember. I don't think so."

"She got pregnant by a German with blue eyes who took off for the war, so Irene, her mother, got big Matt Donofrio to marry her. He was an Italian immigrant, twenty years older, and a jealous maniac. He had a pizza-parlor business on the corner and a taxi-cab business too, but the phone was at their house. If ever he heard somebody had called and Grammy didn't answer, he'd run home, pull her onto the porch, and smack her. He did it in public, because he thought she was screwing with a neighbor."

"Wow," Jason said.

"Those old Italians were lunatics. Big Matt used to be a bootlegger too, and more than once he got hauled down to the station for fighting. Pop said it took three cops to pin him down and that the old-timers on the force used to say to Pop, 'Your old man would turn in his grave if he could see his son in uniform.' But of course, there's not much difference between cops and criminals. Come to think of it, that's three generations, too: Big Matt, Pop, and Uncle Mike."

I wondered if there was a precedent in our family for born-again virgins like me. Come to think of it, there were only two other college graduates in my family, both elementary-school teachers, and they didn't have the most active sex lives. One, my father's sister, didn't get married until she was over thirty, and had a nose that twitched like a rabbit or like she'd just been shocked by an overdose of carbonation; and the other, my father's cousin, never married. She was so wide that whenever she came for a shower or a wedding, she had to sit on two chairs pushed together. Well, I'd never wanted to marry after Raymond, and I supposed I'd had enough sex to last a lifetime, and fact was, I didn't even miss sex itself that much. Maybe what I missed was love.

Then out of the blue, like a siren, Olivia, the one remaining Italian, besides me, in our mostly Puerto Rican building decided she wanted to be my friend and began telling me her life story in installments. Olivia was the real thing, an authentic old maid. She was in her sixties, short, and shaped like a block. Her hair was dyed blue-black and on the street she wore a dramatic black cape that reached her ankles and a tartan red beret. She inevitably had two shopping bags hanging from her hands, maybe for balance. It was the summer before Jason's senior year, when I was about to turn thirty-five, that Olivia decided to open the door to her apartment every time I tried to pass it on the stairs and invite me in for conversation, which meant to tell me the story of her life.

Her apartment was shiny and white and smelled of gas. She had a plastic ivy creeping up her window and plastic birds stapled to the vine. The last time, she didn't even offer me instant coffee before she started talking, kind of breathless like the air was trapped in her chest, and I knew tonight we would get to the point of her story.

"My life," she said, "was ruined. See these ugly black shoes? Orthopedic. Didn't you ever notice the way I walk? Slow, like the clicking of a clock. The kids teased me on our way to school. I could never keep up. Never got married because of my feet. I know three languages, but I never traveled. I gave up religion because I'm so bitter."

I thought this confession would make her start crying, but apparently she'd given that up a long time ago.

That night in bed, I was awakened by the screech of a bird and the hysterical flapping of wings. A sparrow was flailing around my living room, knocking into walls, whacking its head on the ceiling. I couldn't watch it, let alone try to catch it. I called to Jason.

He trapped the bird in the bottom shelf of the book case, then picked it up and held it in his cupped hands. He looked at it for a moment, petted its head with his finger, then put his hand out the window, and the bird flew off.

When I went back to bed, I couldn't sleep. I kept thinking about birds leaving nests. Flying and getting trapped. Beliefs that cripple and hands out windows. Then I thought of Olivia and how her feet had hobbled her life. No. She had hobbled her life with her belief about her feet.

For half of my life, since the day I got pregnant, in fact, I'd thought I'd been stunted by Jason's birth. But that had only been one way to look at it. Another way to look at it would be that the kid enriched my life, and maybe saved me from getting into even more trouble. With a kid to care for, no matter how haphazardly, I had to keep at least one foot on the ground always. This may have been a good thing. Maybe I never would've been given the opportunity to go to college if I hadn't been a mother on welfare. Maybe I would've been feeling much older right now if I hadn't had a kid, because in the act of being forced to grow up so fast, I rebelled and stayed a kid much longer, which contributed to my bohemian life-style (which was dismally out of sync in the middle of the eighties) and my lack of money (ditto), but it had also kept my perspective fresh, my friends the type of women who decide to buy Harley-Davidsons for themselves at the age of forty-five, and a portion of my interest focused on nothing but joy.

Jason ruined my life or he enriched it. My choice. You're just handed some things in life that you have no control over, so you'd better learn from them rather than letting them get you—like Olivia, stewing in bile and bitterness in a stark-white apartment, alone, with birds stapled to her window.

In the morning, before Jason wakes up, I sit in the kitchen with my parents. My father's eating Special K, my mother and I, rye toast. "You're going to miss him," my mother says.

"Yes," I say, not wanting to have this conversation at the same time I'm grateful that somebody's empathizing.

"I remember when your brother went in the service, I cried. Every day. Then when we couldn't contact him, when he was on that secret mission, remember? And finally I called the Red Cross and he called from a staticky phone on some ship? I thought I'd go out of my mind if I didn't hear from him. But at least you won't have to worry about Jason. You know we'll be here if ever he needs anything. I'll probably end up doing his laundry. You know me."

I wonder, not for the first time, if my wanting Jason to go to Wesleyan so badly had not a little to do with the comfort of knowing my parents would only be miles away. I also wondered if, in a way, I was giving him back to them for a while when he was still almost a kid, because we'd always shared the parenting.

"Knowing Jason," my father says, "he'll be home so often you'll get sick of him."

I honestly didn't know if I'd be happy or sad to have him home all the time. But I did know my father was trying to ease the pain. We have a good relationship now. When he retired from the force, he confessed that he'd hated his job for years. Now that he's retired, he builds things: a shed in the backyard, an extra kitchen in the basement; plus, he crochets afghans of clashing colors. He has trouble following directions from the books, so I teach him new stitches when I visit. And we talk about this and that. I realize that some of that time in the years gone by when he was silent, it wasn't because he was mad at me or critical, it was because he was in a bad mood about the politics in his department or some criminal he'd arrested who'd just gotten off scot-free or his life in general.

Our relationship began to change before he retired, though. It was the Christmas after I turned thirty, the same month John Lennon died, which, at the time, I interpreted as the end of youth and the demise of innocence. Now that I was a bona fide adult, I was even more sick and tired than I'd always been of the repetitious obligation of holidays with my family, so I'd resolved to make this visit short. I was arriving on

Christmas Eve and leaving early the next day, nine o'clock in the morning, to go back to the city and spend Christmas with a boyfriend. My mother protested. I insisted. My whole family was pissed, because for the first time in history, we would open our gifts on Christmas Eve, to accommodate me.

My mother woke me up at seven-thirty Christmas morning. I sat in the kitchen with her and my father and spread some cream cheese on a slice of date-nut bread. My mother poured me a cup of coffee and said, "You have a heart of gold." I was used to her saying I had a big head. This heart-of-gold stuff was new to me and it put me on guard. She was saying it because the night before, I'd given my sister Rose one of my gifts. I'd given it to her because I didn't like it.

"No I don't," I said.

"You'd give anybody the shirt off your back," she insisted.

"No I wouldn't," I insisted back.

"Then you've changed," she said. I could've said, No I haven't, but decided to end the game.

My father got up and started putting on his shoes. I told him I didn't need a ride to the station. I'd rather walk.

"You sure? It's cold out," he said.

"I'm sure," I said, looking forward to the solitude.

I kissed Jase on the forehead without waking him, then I left. At the station, I sat on the bench and smoked a roach I'd found in my pocket. A train flew by in the wrong direction. Then there was no other. It was freezing out and I was beginning to get worried. I sat on my hands and jiggled my body. I moved my feet in circles to get them circulating. I looked up. My father was walking toward me.

The first thing I thought was, Good thing I finished

the roach, and the next thing I thought was, Why's he spying on me?

"Thought I'd check to see you got off all right," he said when he got closer.

I knew it was the truth. He hadn't been spying, just concerned. He was a father looking after his daughter. That was the other side of the story. The story of the man worried about the teenage daughter he'd just spotted ducking in the backseat of a passing vehicle full of drunk teenagers. So simple. But to me it was a revelation. Maybe he loved me after all.

He pulled a schedule from his jacket. There wasn't a train for two hours. He offered to drive me to New Haven. We'd have just enough time to make the next one. On the ride to the station, I wanted to talk. To let him know in some way I knew how he felt. To let him know how I felt. But never past the age of four had we talked. How could I start now, on Christmas, during a twenty-minute car ride? He turned on the radio. "Silent Night" came on. I sang. He sang the harmony.

When Jason and I say goodbye to my parents, there are tears in my mother's eyes and I know they're for me, because definitely, by the weekend my father will drive her to Jason's dorm room. She'll give him a banana bread wrapped in tin foil, remark on what a mess his room is, and start picking up his laundry to take home.

In the car heading for Wesleyan, I say, "What do you remember most about living there?"

"The kids," he said. "They taught me to ride a two-wheeler, remember?"

"Uh-huh. Are you nervous now? Afraid it won't be the same as it was?"

"Yeah. Sometimes I think I should've stayed in New York. Gone to Columbia."

"No." I insist, thinking that he'd live in our apartment for four more years, when it was time to make the break. Time to grow up. For both of us. "It'll be good for you to experience the country. Smell the seasons. Live a different life from subways and bars and traffic fumes for a while."

"But people in Connecticut are stupid."

"What?"

"They are."

"You're saying that if we never moved to New York and we stayed in Connecticut we'd be stupid?"

"Yes."

"Oh God. I never in my life ever dreamed I'd raise a snob. People in New York are maybe more sarcastic and quick, but it doesn't make them smarter. Don't kid yourself." I looked at him then. Black jeans, black T-shirt, sneakers, sunglasses. I wondered if he looked like a city slicker. I wondered how he'd get on. If he'd be expecting it to be one way, the way he remembered, and when he found it different, which he surely would, if he'd hate it. Maybe it had been a mistake to try to go back to utopia, but we'd never questioned it, not for a second. I'd promised him from the day we left for New York, and he'd wanted to stay at Wesleyan, that he could go to school there himself, provided he got all A's in high school. So he got a ninety-two-point-something average, and then came running home the fall of his senior year in a panic. "Ma!" he said. "The lowest average Wesleyan accepted from Stuyvesant last year was ninety-four. They'll never give me a scholarship."

This news threw me into a panic too. I'd just finished graduate school myself the year before. I'd been proofreading and copyediting, mostly at my kitchen table. We had no money, as usual. The only schools he could "afford" to go to were extraordinarily expensive schools like Wesleyan, because they were the ones with big endowments. If he had to go to a state school, I didn't know how we'd swing it. But I acted cool. I said, "Well, then we should consider an alternative. Part of the state university system, Cornell, plus another elite school, Yale or Amherst or someplace."

"You promised I could go to Wesleyan. If I don't get in, I'm joining the air force."

"What?"

"We wouldn't have to pay. Plus, I could wear a uniform. I'd fly a fighter jet. I'd carry a gun."

Now I knew what my mother had meant when she said I was killing my father. I felt like three bullets went straight to my heart. So this is what kids of hippies grow up to be: future four-star generals. The next day I was copyediting at a magazine and had to run into the bathroom for a half-hour weep when I started thinking that maybe this was GI Joe residue. Maybe this air force bullshit was all about his father who, after all, had been in the 101st Airborne Division.

When Jason was eleven, he began asking questions. "What does my father look like? Where do you think he lives? Do you think we could find him if we wanted?" At the time, I thought maybe Jason needed his father because of the approach of puberty. I suggested he make a search. He called the one phone number I had, which was his great-grandmother's, in Bangor, Maine. She gave us the number of his grandmother, who refused to give Jase his father's number, probably because she was afraid we were after back alimony and child support. But she did say she'd give our number to Raymond. Raymond called that same afternoon. Jason talked to his father for a minute, saying, "Fine. Sixth grade. Okay. New York. Good." Then he handed the phone to me.

I'd recognize the voice anywhere.

"I hear you been to college. That's good. You always were smart. I been married again. Fucked that up too. Met her after Nam. We got two girls. Then I left. Don't see them neither. You know what they say: Once a fuck-up . . . I got a job. Loading stuff on trucks. Same old shit. I'm living with a lady. She got a baby. It's not bad. So, how's Jason? He a good kid?"

"Yeah," I said, not elaborating, because I wanted off the phone in the worst way.

"I was wondering. What if Jason came for a visit? We live up at Greenwood Lake. It's only two hours by bus. They got one from the Port Authority."

I took Jason to the bus the next weekend. As we stood on line, he said, "How will I know him?"

I'd shown him a picture. "You saw what he looks like."

"What if he doesn't look like that anymore?"

"Don't worry. You'll recognize each other. I know it."

When he came home, he brought a bag of chocolate-chip cookies baked by Raymond's girlfriend. He didn't say much, except that his father lived with a woman who was nice and had a daughter named Juice because she liked it. He said his father was a little fat and they went to bars, where Jason played pinball and Raymond watched television.

His father had given him twenty dollars and a promise to get in touch.

A year later, Jason said, "How much is Social Security?"

"What do you mean?"

"If my father was dead and I got Social Security, how much would it be?"

"I don't know. Maybe two hundred a month."

"How would we know if he died? We should find out. I could get money."

"Jason," I said. "Which would you rather get, a birthday card or Social Security?"

"A birthday card," he said, diverting his eyes to look out the window.

I blew my nose in the bathroom stall at work. I put on fresh lipstick and went back to my desk to take advantage of the WATS line. I called up the air force academy and asked them to send an application. I asked them questions, then called Jason up and used reverse psychology, like in the old days. I said, "They're sending a catalog. They said we'll have to get a senator from this state to recommend you. Did you know they give you physcial training, like in boot camp? It might be good for you. . . ."

"Ma. I was only saying that. You better get me into Wesleyan."

"I better get you in?"

"You promised. You said if I got A's I could go there."

The subtext was that he'd done his part by being a good student and now it was my part as his parent to provide him with college. Hadn't I been furious at my parents for not being able to afford to send me to college? Wasn't this another skip in the record, another generational repeat? He was right. It was partly my responsibility to get my kid to college, but it still pissed me off. I'd just finished getting myself through college, and then graduate school, with no help from parents. And now, to have my kid threaten me with "you betters" and enlistment in the armed forces was too much.

"Get yourself in. It's your life, not mine. You're acting like an idiot."

"You're an idiot."

"Don't you call me an idiot."

He hung up on me.

We hated each other for a couple of days, then eventually started acting like nothing had happened, which was one of our routines.

I knew a great college essay would do the trick. The requested subject was: Describe the person who had the greatest influence on you in your life.

Jase thought he should write about me. Then I came up with a brilliant idea. "What if," I said, "you wrote about the absence of your father."

"Yeah," he said, barely nodding his head. "They'd like that. But that's harder."

"That's what makes it so great."

Jason's dorm room is a single. He has a bed, a bureau, a desk, and a closet. He also has a balcony, which we stand on first thing. "Smell it," I say, talking about the air.

"Nice," he says.

"Look at your view." It's of a hill with pine trees.

"Um-hm," Jase says.

"Well? Isn't it gorgeous?"

"Yes."

I want him to be more enthusiastic. I want him to set me at ease about leaving him here. When we start unpacking, he opens his suitcase and I see that he's jammed everything in without folding. On the top there's a sweater covered with dust and cat hair. I tell him to shake it over the railing and get a guilt pang because I hadn't helped him pack like a normal mother. Next he begins putting his shirts in a drawer.

"Jase," I tell him. "You hang shirts in a closet." The last closet he had was when we lived at Wesleyan. How would he ever fit in? Across the hall, I see a kid unpacking with his parents and his sister. He's hooking up a complex stereo system. There's a computer on his desk. An Indian rug on the wall. Jason has a clock radio and a portable typewriter. His bottom and top sheets don't match.

"Jase," I say. "Look at that kid's room."

"Nice," he says.

"Do you think you're going to feel deprived?"

"What do you mean?"

"A lot of kids are going to be rich. Most of them are going to have more than you. Do you think it'll make you mad or jealous?"

"I don't care about that stuff, and neither do you."

I wasn't talking only about the things. I was talking about the father and sister in addition to the mother. This I don't tell him.

After his room's set up, we ride over to the hockey rink parking lot, where he's supposed to group with two hundred kids to go on a camping trip for a kind of orientation. Our two old houses across the road appear exactly the same. The hockey rink hasn't changed either except for the parents and students milling around eating cookies and drinking lemonade.

When Jase and I reach for some cookies, he floors me by saying, "I wonder if they think you're my girlfriend. You look young for your age and I look old."

It's not that I hadn't wondered the same thing

about a million times. For the past couple of years, whenever we'd walked together or gone out to eat, people looked at him, then at me, like I was an older woman with a younger man, not a mother with her son. But I'd had no idea Jase had been aware of this too.

"Does it bother you?" I ask him.

"No. I think it's cool."

After he says this, I have to admit to myself I do too.

We take our cookies and lemonade and instead of socializing like we're supposed to, we sit on a hill, our arms touching, watching. In the summer that just passed, Jase and I spent many nights at the Polish bar, sitting on barstools, drinking Cokes or beers, watching. One night, a guy I'd begun seeing surprised me by dropping by. When I introduced him to Jason, Jase stood up and shook his hand, then offered him his stool. When my friend went to the bathroom, Jase said, "He's a nice guy, Mom. I like him. When he comes back, I'll stay for a minute, then leave so you can be alone."

"You don't have to."

"I don't mind."

Jason was being chivalrous. He was being a friend, and he was giving me permission to have a boyfriend. It made me very happy at the same time it made me want to hug him and keep him near. Our days as a couple were coming to a close.

Kids were beginning to form lines near the buses. "Maybe it's time for me to go?" I ask.

"Yeah," he says.

When we get to the car he opens the door for me. I hug him for what seems like a long time but is probably short. I say, "I love you."

"I love you too," he says. His eye kind of twitches and I hope with all my heart he doesn't start crying.

I resist the urge to look for him in the rearview. By the time I reach my first stop sign, I'm sobbing so hard I have to pull to the side of the road. It occurs to me that I have never felt so alone in my life. I make a turn that points me in the direction of Wallingford, and when I see the old reservoir approaching I feel much calmer. I decide to spend the evening at my parents', but once I reach the entrance to the interstate I've changed my mind. I turn south, and go home.

FOR THE BEST IN PAPERBACKS, LOOK FOR THE

In every corner of the world, on every subject under the sun, Penguin represents quality and variety—the very best in publishing today.

For complete information about books available from Penguin—including Puffins, Penguin Classics, and Compass—and how to order them, write to us at the appropriate address below. Please note that for copyright reasons the selection of books varies from country to country.

In the United Kingdom: Please write to *Dept. EP, Penguin Books Ltd, Bath Road, Harmondsworth, West Drayton, Middlesex UB7 0DA.*

In the United States: Please write to *Penguin Putnam Inc., P.O. Box 12289 Dept. B, Newark, New Jersey 07101-5289* or call 1-800-788-6262.

In Canada: Please write to *Penguin Books Canada Ltd, 10 Alcorn Avenue, Suite 300, Toronto, Ontario M4V 3B2.*

In Australia: Please write to *Penguin Books Australia Ltd, P.O. Box 257, Ringwood, Victoria 3134.*

In New Zealand: Please write to *Penguin Books (NZ) Ltd, Private Bag 102902, North Shore Mail Centre, Auckland 10.*

In India: Please write to *Penguin Books India Pvt Ltd, 11 Panchsheel Shopping Centre, Panchsheel Park, New Delhi 110 017.*

In the Netherlands: Please write to *Penguin Books Netherlands bv, Postbus 3507, NL-1001 AH Amsterdam.*

In Germany: Please write to *Penguin Books Deutschland GmbH, Metzlerstrasse 26, 60594 Frankfurt am Main.*

In Spain: Please write to *Penguin Books S. A., Bravo Murillo 19, 1° B, 28015 Madrid.*

In Italy: Please write to *Penguin Italia s.r.l., Via Benedetto Croce 2, 20094 Corsico, Milano.*

In France: Please write to *Penguin France, Le Carré Wilson, 62 rue Benjamin Baillaud, 31500 Toulouse.*

In Japan: Please write to *Penguin Books Japan Ltd, Kaneko Building, 2-3-25 Koraku, Bunkyo-Ku, Tokyo 112.*

In South Africa: Please write to *Penguin Books South Africa (Pty) Ltd, Private Bag X14, Parkview, 2122 Johannesburg.*